Provided

by

Measure B

which was approved

by the voters in

November, 1998

FASHIONS
OF THE
PAST

FASHIONS
OF THE
PAST

•

FOREWORD BY
DR AILEEN RIBEIRO
HEAD OF THE HISTORY OF DRESS DEPARTMENT
COURTAULD INSTITUTE OF ART

•

ANNA BURUMA

COLLINS & BROWN

Illustrations previously published in Costumes of All Nations, by The First Munich Artists, London, 1901 (1st edition) and 1907 (3rd edition).

This edition first published in Great Britain in 1999 by
Collins & Brown Limited
London House, Great Eastern Wharf
Parkgate Road, London SW11 4NQ

Distributed in the United States and Canada by Sterling Publishing Co.,
387 Park Avenue South, New York, NY 10016

1 3 5 7 9 8 6 4 2

A CIP record for this book is available from the British Library

ISBN 1 85585 7278 (hardback edition)
ISBN 1 85585 7286 (paperback edition)

Editor Elizabeth Drury
Design Paul Vater at Sugar Free

Reproduction by Grasmere Digital
Printed in China

FASHIONS OF THE PAST

contents

DR AILEEN RIBEIRO
HEAD OF THE HISTORY OF DRESS SECTION, COURTAULD INSTITUTE OF ART

T he late nineteenth century was a golden age for the publication of encyclopaedic books of costume plates. In a way it was the last flowering of the Renaissance tradition of *Trachtenbücher* – compilations of costume illustrations – testifying to a growing interest in the wider world that was fostered by travel, trade and exploration. The early costume books had the minimum of text, but the illustrations – woodcuts, engravings or, less often, watercolours – gave enough detailed visual information on clothing to be of practical help to artists and to the designers of the theatrical spectacles, pageantry and court entertainments that were so popular at the period.

The illustrations in this book are taken from the *Costumes of All Nations*, published in Britain in 1901 and 1907, a selection of the plates first published in *Münchener Bilderbogen* between 1848 and 1898. This aimed to be a comprehensive visual survey of historic dress from the ancient civilizations to the early nineteenth century. The focus was on diversity, and the accomplished artists commissioned for this ambitious series of costume vignettes depicted not just the chronology of fashion but a range of types of dress according to rank, status and occupation: armour, uniform, religious vestments, for example, feature along with illustrations of the élite and the middle classes, and the regional dress that the nineteenth century found so picturesque. The plates tell the story of fashion from the standpoint that is familiar to the western European dress historian, a history of costume based on that of France, England, Italy and the Netherlands. But we also get a much wider view, a world outlook, a kind of sartorial *Weltanschauung*.

Of the many strands that make up the history of costume, those of geography, nationality and ethnic diversity have sometimes been overlooked in a discussion of mainstream developments. They figure here, however, and raise a number of questions. Does geography or the concept of

French lady and gentleman, 1780.

nationhood influence dress? How far does costume, like language, become an emblem of national consciousness? How did the distinctive styles of regional or folk costume develop? This book reminds us that Germany played a pivotal role in Europe and that it was once at the heart of a large empire. At the centre of Europe, it was an axis around which were situated a bewildering network of small nations, from the Baltic to the Balkans, whose ethnic variety was recognized through costume. Germany's own internal diversity, as the book makes clear, could be seen in the very different costumes of its regions and city-states, partly the result of sumptuary laws, partly dictated by tradition.

Fashions of the Past ranges widely both historically and geographically. The plates cover not just Europe but beyond – from Turkey, to the Middle East, to India and the Far East, to Africa. Some of the interest in faraway places must have been caused by German attempts to found a colonial empire, but also from a fascination with the new science of anthropology. Germany was one of the leaders in serious archaeological research and this, too, is reflected, in the sections dealing with the costume of ancient civilizations.

This edition serves to introduce the *Münchener Bilderbogen* to a wider audience. Recognition is richly deserved, for the plates are of high quality and taken from a wide range of visual sources – Classical sculpture, wall-paintings, illuminated manuscripts, early costume books, fashion plates and portraits. Inevitably, especially for periods from which no costume survives, there are errors of interpretation. There are also figures that have been given late nineteenth-century poses and attitudes, presenting a kind of self-conscious solemnity (and unconscious humour) that was very much part of the aesthetic of the time and that has a certain period charm. On the whole, however, the plates are a faithful record of what the artists saw in the original works of art. They are detailed enough for the modern designer to find useful, giving a sense of the colour and appearance of costume both ancient and modern.

The present selection rearranges the plates into chronologies and themes. Each chapter has a useful introduction that sets the illustrations in context and describes what we see. Such a wonderful source book of costume images is not only useful as a survey of world dress – and as an indication of how historic and contemporary costume was seen at the end of the nineteenth century – but is a work of art in its own right.

The Byzantine Emperor Justinian (483–565) and The Empress Theodora (?508–48).

Introduction

BY ANNA BURUMA

Woman from Munich, first half of 17th century. The illustrations were first published in Munich, between 1848 and 1898.

The plates in *Fashions from the Past*, which come from the series *Münchener Bilderbogen*, belong to a long publishing tradition that dates back to the last quarter of the sixteenth century. At that time a number of printed books illustrated with costume images appeared, images that have played an important part in the study of dress history throughout the succeeding centuries.

The role of printing in the sixteenth century can be compared to that of the media of the present day. Printed material provided education and entertainment, and was just as full of trivia. Everything and anything was pictured in print, stock images being used and reused in ways that were sometimes appropriate and sometimes inappropriate. As with modern television programming, enormous attention was paid to far-off places. Maps, topographical plates, travel accounts and journals of explorations were published that were evidence of the demand at that time for information about newly discovered parts of the world. Pamphlets and broadsheets were produced on life in Russia, on Japanese princes visiting Italy as well as on the people found living on Baffin Island, some of whom were brought back by the explorers as 'specimens'.

Editions of these pamphlets and broadsheets could run into the hundreds, and they were copied constantly for publication in different cities. As now, because of the multiplication of descriptions and images, inaccuracies and prejudices would often become 'truths'. National stereotypes emerged and stuck. Germans for example were always described as drunkards, and Dutch women were always praised for their clean linen.

Early costume books belong among this type of material. They were aimed at various audiences, including collectors of curiosities. The introductions to some of these books stated that they were also meant for travellers, engineers, businessmen, statesmen, architects and artists. Artists were in the practice of using prints as reference for their own work, and surviving inventories show us that some artists, Rembrandt among them, also owned books of costume plates. Theatre companies left inventories showing that they, too, made use of costume books. Most of the sixteenth-century books illustrated dress from around the world and were not intended to provide a history of costume. Cesare Vecellio's *De gli habiti antichi, et moderni et diverse parti del mondo*, of 1590, was an exception. Typically, he trawled through all the previously published books and used images from them, but he was unique in including the costume of previous centuries.

The books continued to be produced in the early seventeenth century, but they were often reprints of sixteenth-century ones, or else they concentrated on the dress of a particular city such as Venice, as instanced by Giacomo Franco in his *Habiti d'huomini et donne venetiane* of 1609. Later in the seventeenth century, there were many single prints and several series of prints showing dress, but no books. Jacques Callot, Abraham Bosse and Jean de St-Igny in France, and the de Bry family, Romeyn De Hooghe, Jacob de Gheyn and others in the Low Countries, all produced engravings with dress as the main subject.

Florentine woman, 1581. The figure was based on one in Habitus variatum orbis gentium *by Jean Jacques Boissard.*

In the mid-seventeenth century, one of the most important artists to portray the dress of various different regions was the Bohemian Wenceslaus Hollar, images from whose *Theatre of Women* of 1643 are still referred to today. In the third quarter of the century a periodical putting together words and images of fashion was published in Paris, the *Mercure Galant*. However, fashion plates did not really come into their own until the following century.

In the eighteenth century, there was a renewed interest in costume books, from ones showing regional dress to ones showing costumes from around the world. The books illustrating figures from exotic lands were much used in the thriving masquerade costume business. It was during the eighteenth century that an antiquarian interest in dress emerged. One of the first books in the field was *Monuments de la monarchie françoise* by

Bernard de Montfaucon, published in 1729–33. His brother, Le Prévot, became a pioneer in the study of prehistory after a prehistoric tomb was found on his estate in Normandy. In England, the first serious study of the history of dress was by Joseph Strutt, the *Compleat View of the Manners, Customs, Arms, Habits etc. of the Inhabitants of England*, published in 1774–6.

In the early nineteenth century, there was a proliferation of rather more popular books on the subject. Historical accuracy was thought too stuffy and instead books promised to bring the past alive in a different and more amusing way. It was not until the second half of the century that a more serious approach was taken up again, notably in James Planché's *Cyclopedia of Costume Dictionary of Dress* (1876–9), and Albert Racinet's *Le costume historique* (1876–88).

French abbé, *1770–85. The figure was based on an ewngraving after Moreau le Jeune, published in* Monument du Costume.

In 1848, Braun & Schneider issued the first number of the *Münchener Bilderbogen*, a series of plates on various subjects published singly every fortnight. Between 1848 and 1898, 1200 plates in all were published, and between 1902 and 1929 a further thirty-one plates appeared sporadically. From the beginning, the *Bilderbogen* appealed to popular taste. Other such series had existed earlier in the century, but most were of a fairly low quality and the artwork not particularly good.

There was an art academy in Munich and therefore there were many impecunious young artists. Braun and Schneider were wily businessmen and would pay a small lump sum for any artwork provided. The artists had to sign away all rights to the work they sold. Many artists left as soon as they had made their name and, by the end, nearly 200 artists had contributed to the *Bilderbogen*. As bound annuals, the plates became affordable picture books, and they are regarded as an important influence on children's literature. Such well-known German classics as Carl Reinhardt's *Kasperl* and Wilhelm Busch's *Max und Moritz* owe their origins to these publications.

At the end of the 1850s, Braun & Schneider created several educational series within the regular *Bilderbogen: Die Welt in Bildern* (The World in Pictures), *Bilder aus dem Alterthume* (Pictures from Ancient Times) and *Zur Geschichte der Kostüme* (On the

History of Costume). All three series, equivalent to the modern part-work on a single subject, were offered to schools. The costume plates acquired the greatest following. In addition to their use in schools, fashion magazines recommended them to their readers, both to help them brighten up their wardrobes and to serve as inspiration for carnival costumes. Artists are known to have bought the *Bilderbogen* to copy in their own work, as was the tradition. The first numbers of the costume series appeared in 1861, and the last twelve were issued between 1903 and 1905. In the end a total of 125 numbers were published. The plates were also published in Britain in book form under the title *Costumes of All Nations*, in 1901 and 1907.

Braun & Schneider's costume images provided a new historical accuracy. The artists went back to original sources and copied from funerary monuments, mosaics, frescoes, portraits and photographs, and from examples of dress in museums. Some of the sources used by the illustrators were well known – the Byzantine mosaics in Ravenna and Holbein's portrait of Henry VIII – others were less accessible: for instance, they looked at medieval manuscripts in the State Library in Munich and visited ethnographic museums to draw the regional costumes.

Henry VIII, 1520s. The figure was based on a portrait by Hans Holbein.

In 1873, there was a major Ottoman exhibition in Vienna. Costumes from various parts of the Empire were put on show, and a large album was produced that demonstrated the manner in which the costumes were worn. The photographs for the album were taken by Pascal Sébah, using non-Muslim models. They were probably the source of the nineteenth-century Ottoman illustrations not only in Braun & Schneider's publication but also in Racinet's book.

Some of the costume illustrations are less reliable than others, particularly in the chapters on the early civilizations. It should be remembered that archaeological discoveries were being made almost daily at the time the work was being published. Schliemann was discovering the treasures at Troy in 1870; the Assyrian palaces were found in the 1840s, and the most important excavations of Babylon by Koldewey were undertaken in 1899. Carter did not find Tutankhamen's tomb until later, in 1922. Some of the most up-to-date knowledge did find its way into the illustrations. For example, information from the Jutland excavations in Scandinavia between 1871 and 1875 resulted in the publication in 1888 of a plate of the Bronze Age Teutons.

Unlike the works of Planché and Racinet, there was no text with the *Bilderbogen* images. However, the illustrations, done by various different hands, were on the whole beautifully executed. Braun & Schneider had reason to be proud that they managed to maintain such a high standard in a field where so many did not.

There were 125 costume plates in all, and about half of them have been selected for *Fashions of the Past*. They have been arranged by geographical area, following the example of the sixteenth-century books on costume. As the illustrations were created in Germany, it is not surprising to find that there are far more German images than of any other nation. In the present selection a balance has been attempted, but proportionately, there is still a high percentage of German illustrations. Many of the sixteenth-century books added a section in the back on religious dress, and the same has been done here. The early historic plates had few precedents in the early books but, surprisingly, examples of northern and southern American dress were included; none from these parts of the world appeared in Braun & Schneider's series, however.

Austrian infantryman, 1760–75. Illustrations of soldiers appear among those showing civilian dress.

The illustrations of soldiers have been placed within their geographical areas in order to make the point that civilian dress did not develop in isolation but influenced, and was influenced by, military dress, including armour. The series illustrated much regional dress. As the Industrial Revolution progressed during the nineteenth century, old traditions disappeared. With this came a desire to preserve a nation's cultural identity, and folk music, dancing, stories and artifacts were recorded and collected. An interest in regional dress was another aspect of this movement. Some of the items of dress had genuinely developed over the centuries, but some were newly created as an expression of the new nationalism.

The historian Fernand Braudel remarked that an understanding of fashions and changing styles in dress involves a study of the availability of raw materials, production processes, manufacturing costs, cultural stability, fashion and social hierarchy. The arrangement of the illustrations in this book shows clearly how the different regions co-existed. Through trade, war and population movements, the various cultures have continuously intermingled and developed, and this has had an enormous influence on the use of particular textiles and types of dress. It is interesting to see how the Silk Road, for example, gave the central Asian nomads an important role in the distribution of textiles and dissemination of styles of dress in both East and West, and over a long period. Water routes, both at sea and by river, were important too in the trading patterns between North and South. The caftan, the trousers and the tunic replacing draped clothing in different areas shows how far and where those lines of communication led. The use of the various textiles had a profound effect on the economy of the regions, and also on the form of the clothes.

The history of dress has always been in danger of being exclusively about the élite because of the availability of information, but understanding the role of the peasant in growing the raw materials, and the labouring and middle classes in manufacturing and trading in the final product, is vital. Without their involvement there would have been far less change in fashionable dress. Weavers were essentially self-employed and better educated than most workers, and they had a sense of independence. With the Reformation in the sixteenth century, they were naturally attracted to the idea of self-determination, and they enthusiastically embraced Protestantism. This was to have important repercussions in the various economies of Europe as many were forced to leave their own regions for a suitable religious climate in England, Germany and the Netherlands.

Travel, through emigration for religious reasons, for trade, for war or for pleasure, truly broadens people's experience and outlook. Foreign dress was always of interest, sometimes as a curiosity and often as a source of inspiration for design. This was the appeal of the original plates reproduced here, and so it is in their newly published form in *Fashions of the Past*, now with an informative accompanying text.

Chinese merchant from Penang, second half of 19th century. This is one of the latest in date of the costume illustrations.

Ancient Civilizations

The civilizations described in this chapter were to the east of and around the Mediterranean: Mesopotamia, Egypt, Greece and Rome.

The early settlers in the Near and Middle East cultivated different plants – hemp, rush, papyrus, palm and, especially, flax – while sheep and goats were domesticated by both the settled communities and the nomads of these regions; thus they were provided with both linen and wool for clothes, furnishings and tents.

There was a knowledge of dye techniques from early on, and plants, insects and other creatures were used to produce different colours: the famous 'purple', which was in fact a reddish colour, came from the small mollusc murex.

Various cultures originated at different times in Mesopotamia, the region between the rivers Tigris and Euphrates, roughly where modern Iraq now is. Favourable conditions meant that people settled there from around 10,000 BC. The Sumerians, whose civilization was at its peak in the third millennium BC, occupied the region from about 5000 BC. The Sumerians (and the Akkadians, a Semitic people who next dominated the region) had sheepskin skirts and cloaks, and later similar garments of woven wool, often with a looped ground to simulate the wool of the sheepskin. Felted wool, linen and leather were also worn.

The Babylonians and later the Assyrians ruled from around the twenty-first century to the sixth century BC. Babylonian and Assyrian men and women wore two basic garments: a tunic, and a fringed and tasselled shawl held in place by a wide belt. Wool was still the material used most frequently. It was usually dyed in bright colours and decorated with geometric patterns.

The history of the Jews began in the second millennium BC with Abraham, whose family came from near Ur, a city at the mouth of the Euphrates. Their textiles and clothes would have been similar to those of the Babylonians and Assyrians and, being nomads, these would have been made mainly of wool.

The great Egyptian periods can be divided very roughly into the Old Kingdom (*c.* 2700–2200 BC), the Middle Kingdom (*c.* 2100–1800 BC) and the New Kingdom (*c.* 1600–1100 BC). Wall-paintings, sculptures and ceramics show the kind of clothes the Egyptians wore, and, because plant fibres survive well in dry desert conditions, actual garments also survive. The Egyptians had mainly linen garments, but it is known that sheep's and goat's wool, and bark, were also used for clothing.

Linen is difficult to dye, and the Old Kingdom Egyptians preferred their clothes to be a white. The linen garments were decorated in other ways, by bleaching, pleating, and even embroidery and beading. They used quite complicated pleating techniques, in which the linen was stiffened and pleated in horizontal, vertical and herringbone patterns. During the

Jewish high priest,
c. 6th century BC–
1st century AD.

(background image)
Greek women,
6th–5th century BC.

New Kingdom, coloured cloths were woven. Egyptian dress consisted of both wrapped and sewn garments. The Egyptians had metal and bone needles, and were able to do very fine work. Sewn garments were usually rectangles stitched along one or more sides, and would be fastened with lacing.

Ancient Greece can be divided into three main periods too: the Archaic, which runs from the seventh to the fifth century BC, the Classical, from the fifth to the fourth century BC, and the Hellenistic, during the third and second centuries BC. Greek dress consisted of four basic garments: the *peplos, chiton, himation* and *chlamys*. The Dorian *peplos* was a simple form of dress worn by all Greek women up to the sixth century BC and revived after the Persian wars (480 BC). Made of wool, it would be dyed and often patterned. A cloth, with its upper edge folded over, was wrapped around the body, and caught together at each shoulder by large pins and hitched up over a belt. The Ionic *chiton*, worn from 600 BC, was a tunic made of a cloth folded in two or of two separate pieces. While the *peplos* was of wool, the *chiton* was always of linen or cotton. Over the *peplos* and the *chiton*, the *himation*, or cloak, could be worn. Men in the early periods wore just a *himation*; later, a short *chiton* would be worn underneath. The *chlamys* was a smaller cloak worn by younger men. The garments were formed from rectangles of material and were always woven to size by women. Items such as hooded cloaks, leg coverings and Phrygian caps came from the East. As trading expanded eastwards, cottons came from India and silks from China.

The Roman domination began in the third century BC. By the second century AD, the Roman Empire extended from Spain to the Black Sea and from Britain to Egypt. Roman dress followed the Greek model, but with differences: whereas Greek clothes were made of simple rectangles, Roman dress often had curved lines, and some cutting and sewing were involved. Greek geometric patterning made way for more complicated shapes.

The toga is the best-known Roman garment. Inherited from an Etruscan garment called the *tebenna*, it consisted of a huge woollen semi-circular cloth. It might take up to half an hour to drape it properly, and it was important to get the correct curve at the front. Early on, both men and women wore it over a tunic; later, it could only be worn by a Roman (male) citizen. Roman women wore a long tunic of fine linen or wool called a *stola*, which could be with or without sleeves. With sleeves, it was fastened at the shoulders and along the upper arms by small brooches, and belted in the same way as the Greek *chiton*. Over the *stola* lay the *palla*, which could be draped over the head, although it was still essential to wear a veil or other head-covering outdoors. Although these civilizations were the ancestors of Western culture, we shall see that modern Western dress developed from a different model.

Egyptian pharaoh *c.* 1575–1200 BC (top left); *tunica* of a Roman general; 2nd century AD (top right); Assyrian high priest, *c.* 9th–7th century BC (bottom).

ANCIENT CIVILIZATIONS

THREE EGYPTIAN WOMEN

• *c.* 1575–1200 BC

The women are probably from the time of the New Kingdom. Whereas before this period clothes had generally been made from undyed linen, they were now regularly made from coloured cloth. Dress was altogether more decorated than previously. Techniques such as embroidery and appliqué were used, with beads, sequins and braids being sewn on.

Women's dress consisted of a length of cloth that could be wrapped and pinned or sewn into a tube-shaped tunic called a *kalasiris*. These tunics varied in width and length, and were usually pleated. Over the first, heavier one, they often wore a second, more ornate one, with a strap over the left shoulder. A decorative girdle and a mantle with an embroidered edge covering the shoulders completed the outfit.

Jewellery included collars, armbands, bracelets, earrings, fillets, diadems and rings made of glass and faience beads, semi-precious stones and gold. Wigs were usually large and decorative, often indicating rank. Some women added braids to their own hair instead of wearing a wig.

PHARAOH AND TWO ATTENDANTS

• *c.* 1575–1200 BC

The *kalasiris* was worn by men as well as women at the time of the New Kingdom. It could be sleeveless with a shoulder strap, or with a short sleeve to one arm, and it was often worn very short. The skirts varied considerably. A thin pleated outer skirt was worn over an underskirt. Later in the period, the outer skirt was tucked away to reveal a long puffed underskirt, which was often fringed. A mantle made of wool or pleated linen was worn over the *kalasiris*. As with the women, the mantle was often gathered at the centre front, creating the appearance of pleated sleeves. Dress was the same for all classes, but, the wealthier the wearer, the more layers he had on, and the quality of the cloth was better.

The pharaoh's headdress in the illustration is known as the 'two powerful ones'; it consists of the white tiara, or *atef*, of Upper Egypt and the red crown of Lower Egypt. A sacred object, it was kept in the temple. Crowns were often decorated with the rearing viper as a symbol of royalty, and with the *Ankh* cross as a sign of life. Dignitaries accompanying the pharaoh carried a staff or sceptre signifying the support of heaven.

ASSYRIAN KING AND HIGH PRIEST

• *c.* 9TH–7TH CENTURY BC

The figures may be based on reliefs and sculptures from the palaces at Nimrud and Nineveh. The dress of priests was of bleached linen; that of the king would be coloured. The high priest's headdress was decorated with bullock's horns. The basic garment was the shirt, worn by everyone. A priest's dress came in various forms: spiral, with a triangular fringed piece rolled spirally around the body over the shirt, and the point brought over the right shoulder to the belt; and aproned, with an ankle-length apron worn around the back of the body, fastening with hanging tasselled cords and exposing the hem of the short shirt in front. The priest also wore a cloak. Here he appears to be wearing a combination of these two forms.

The king's dress consisted of a long shirt of decorated cloth, either brocaded or embroidered, with tassels and fringes. A royal mantle was worn over the shirt. The wearer's social position was indicated by the number and size of his scarves and mantles, and by the width of the fringes. The king's headdress was a white conical-shaped tiara with a spiked top; the two narrow purple tabs hanging down the back were called *infulae*. Much jewellery was worn. In contrast to all the decoration above, plain sandals were worn on the feet.

ASSYRIAN SOLDIERS

• *c.* 9TH–7TH CENTURY BC

Common soldiers wore a short shirt with a wide protective belt, and quilted leggings and boots. Officers had a cuirass made of a short leather shirt covered with bronze plates; a metal plate at the centre front held together the straps crossing the breast. They wore fringed scarves, and fringed and tasselled aprons over the cuirass. The Assyrian conical helmet at some stage gained a crest. It was made first of copper, then bronze, and finally of iron. The shield could be oblong or round, and was made of bronze.

Like the Egyptians, the Assyrians wore wigs and false beards. The form of the beards indicated rank: kings and high officials had long and elaborately curled beards; soldiers either wore short beards or none at all. Great care was taken over hair and beards. They were curled, dyed and treated with perfumed ointments, and, for special occasions, might be covered with gold dust.

ANCIENT CIVILIZATIONS

JEWISH HIGH PRIEST AND LEVITES

• *c.* 6TH CENTURY BC–1ST CENTURY AD

Apart from his headdress, a Jewish high priest's dress was similar to that worn by the Assyrians. He had linen breeches worn low on the waist. A long-sleeved tunic was put on over this and reached to the ankles. A wide sash woven with a multi-coloured floral pattern was wound twice round the body and tied high on the chest, the ends of it hanging down to the ankles. A blue floor-length sleeveless tunic with gold bells and tassels attached to the bottom edge was put on next. Over this went the *ephod*, a sleeved tunic, which was multi-coloured with gold embroidery.

A brooch was pinned on each shoulder. A breastplate, the *hoshen*, set with twelve stones and with gold chains and cords, was tied in place with blue ribbons and a girdle. The headdress consisted of a linen fillet, encircling the head, with a turban-shaped linen headdress and over this a blue headdress with gold embroidery; a conical gold crown on top was encircled by a gold fillet bearing the name of God in Hebrew.

ROMAN STANDARD-BEARER AND GENERAL

• 2ND CENTURY AD

A standard-bearer, or *signifer*, resembling this figure can be seen on Trajan's Column in Rome (*c.* AD 113). The standard with an eagle mounted on a castle above various plaques and wreaths was adopted in the second century BC. The bearer is dressed as an ordinary soldier but with a bearskin tied around the neck by the front paws, the bear's head resting on the soldier's head.

The general in the picture is wearing a brass or bronze cuirass moulded over a leather doublet, with metal-studded straps protecting the tops of the legs and arms. These are worn over a *tunica*. As a general in command, he wears the semi-circular mantle known as the *paludamentum*. Footwear could be boots or, as here, sandals with straps up the lower leg. The helmet at his feet has movable pieces to protect the forehead and chin; the crest is horsehair, which was often dyed red.

GREEK SOLDIERS

• *c.* 6TH–5TH CENTURY BC

The *Hoplites*, the heavily armed infantry, was the most important division of the Greek army. The typical equipment of an officer would consist of the breastplate, or *thorex*, which was a cloth corselet with metal plates fastened to it; this was worn tight over the tunic and held in place by leather shoulder straps. Below the waist was the *pteryges*, a protective skirt made of stiffened linen.

Common soldiers and archers wore a leather cuirass, a metal belt, greaves and a helmet. The helmet being carried appears from its shape to be Corinthian: surrounding the face and with eye-slits, it was often painted and crested. The helmet on the ground, crested and with hinged side-plates, may be Athenian. The shield is round, with handles on the inside. Shields would usually have a badge or device on the front. Bronze greaves cover the lower legs. The mantle, or *chlamys*, was often wound around the arm to ward off blows.

ROMAN SOLDIERS

• 2ND CENTURY AD

The armour of the Romans was influenced by Greek armour. One of the soldiers is wearing body armour consisting of metal scales fixed to a protective garment of leather or coarse linen, the skirt of which is slit into knee-length straps. This is worn over the basic *tunica*. In colder climates, soldiers wore leggings called *bracae*, a fashion they adopted from the Barbarians.

The soldier on the right has body armour with shoulder pieces made of a series of bronze or iron hoops that slide over each other to give flexibility. The helmet is basin-shaped with a piece to protect the nape of the neck and with cheek flanges. These were fastened under the chin to secure the helmet. The crest of horsehair was usually dyed bright red. The ordinary soldiers carried shields made of wood or wicker-work covered with leather and trimmed with iron. Their names and the number of their legion would be painted on them. Soldiers did not wear armour within the limits of Rome.

ANCIENT CIVILIZATIONS

GREEK WOMEN

• 6TH–5TH CENTURY BC

The three women are wearing the two different forms of Greek female dress: the *peplos* and the *chiton*. The woman in the centre wears a *peplos*, which was worn by all Greek women up to the sixth century BC and was revived in the late fifth century BC. It was a rectangle of wool with the upper edge folded over, the top edges being caught together on each shoulder by long pins, leaving the arms uncovered. It could be bloused over the girdle that held it in place. The garment grew wider, and the overfold so large, that it was often tucked into the girdle or hung over to conceal it.

The woman on the right is probably wearing a *chiton*. This was made of two pieces, which were sewn together down the arm to form sleeves and down the right side. It was often pleated, and women wore it long. Generally it was girdled low in the fifth century BC and high under the breast in the second century BC. Both sexes wore it girdled across the breast. The mantle, or *himation*, was a wool square with its corners weighted. It was draped over one shoulder, which left the other arm free. It often had decorative edges and could be left its natural colour or dyed. Jewellery was worn much more by women than by men. It included pins and brooches, necklaces, earrings, rings, hairpins of ivory, bone and gold, and diadems and fillets.

ROMAN WOMEN

• 2ND CENTURY AD

Female dress in Rome was very like that worn by the Greeks. The long fine linen or wool garment was like the *chiton*, now called the *stola*. Underneath the *stola* was the *tunica interior*, or under-tunic, cut on the same lines. The *stola* could have sleeves, which were fastened with brooches along the arms; if it was sleeveless, the undergarment had sleeves. It was often girdled twice, once under the breast and again around the hips.

The *himation*, draped in a variety of ways over the *stola*, was now called the *palla*. The *palla*, like the *himation*, was of wool. It was often pulled over the head when the wearer was out of doors even though a respectable woman would have a veil or other head-covering.

Roman women wore boots out of doors and sandals in the house. Hair at first was worn simply, but during the Empire it became more elaborate as seen in the central figure. The tightly curled front hair was probably arranged on a frame.

GREEK VICTOR IN OLYMPIAN GAMES, PRIEST AND KING

• 6TH–5TH CENTURY BC

Before women began wearing it, the *chiton* was a man's garment. It would be worn long by elderly men or on ceremonial occasions, but active men wore it mid-thigh. It was made of linen, and was always woven to size. Workers sometimes wore a *chiton* caught on one shoulder for greater freedom of movement. Theirs was often made of sheepskin or leather.

A *chiton* on its own was informal, and a cloak such as the *himation* or the *chlamys* would be worn with it. The *chlamys* was a smaller woollen rectangle, sometimes with a border. The *himation* or *chlamys* was sometimes worn without the *chiton*, and in this case it was often large enough to cover the figure down to the feet. The simplest method of arranging the *himation* or the *chlamys* was to throw it over the shoulders letting the ends hang loose. The short *chlamys* could be fastened on the right shoulder. Until the fourth century BC, men did not shave, except for philosophers and scholars, who wore beards.

ROMAN EMPEROR, LICTOR AND GENTLEMAN

• 2ND CENTURY AD

The toga was the mark of a Roman citizen. A large semi-circular woollen cloth, it derived from an Etruscan garment called the *tebenna*. There were many ways of draping the toga, and it was important to arrange the correct curve at the front.

The ordinary Roman citizen wore a *toga pura*, which was plain. Magistrates and youths under sixteen wore a *toga praetexta*, which was white with a band of purple or scarlet along the straight edge. Under the toga men wore the Roman *chiton*, called the *tunica*, which could be with or without sleeves. Roman emperors wore the *tunica palmata*, which was embroidered in gold on purple silk. Over this they wore the *toga picta*. In the second century AD, this became part of the official dress of Roman consuls.

The *lictor*, on the left, has a simple *tunica* with an *abolla*, a rectangular woollen cloak, worn double and fastened with a brooch on the right shoulder. It was worn by army officers. On his shoulder he carries the bundle of rods, called the *fasces*, signifying the magistrate's power over life and death.

Early Christian

Christianity may have been introduced into Egypt as early as 41 AD, during St Mark's first visit there. Archaeological evidence indicates that certainly by the middle of the second century there were Christians in the Nile Valley. By the fourth century, persecution of Christians ceased, and at the end of the century eighty per cent of the population is thought to have been Christian. They were known as Coptic Christians.

Egypt became part of the Byzantine Empire, which at its height covered an area from the Black Sea to the north African coast, together with southern Spain, Italy and Greece. Under Byzantine rule, a tense relationship developed between Alexandria and Constantinople. These were the largest cities in this part of the world, but eventually, with the growth of Constantinople, the importance of Alexandria declined. The Byzantines had difficulty defending their territories from their power base in Constantinople, and in 632 AD the prophet Mohammed declared a holy Islamic war against Byzantium, and Egypt was conquered ten years later by the Arabs.

Textiles were an important product of the empire. Constantinople produced fine silks from the fourth century onwards. Before, the raw silk for these fabrics had come from China, but, by the fifth century, Byzantium began to produce its own. Imperial workshops were established in Constantinople itself, and in Egypt and Syria. Alexandria became a major centre for textiles, with fine linen and tapestry weaving as its speciality.

Byzantine dress developed from late Roman dress. The *tunica* had been the basic garment in Rome, worn both indoors and outdoors. Outside the house, the toga was put on over the *tunica*. It was a complicated garment to wear and was eventually replaced by other wraps. The *pallium* was one of these, a long cloak that fastened on the left shoulder with a brooch. Other shorter mantles such as the *chlamys* and the hooded *paenula* were also worn. The dalmatic was originally a male outer garment and had become a common garment in Rome by the third century. It was cut like a *tunica* but wider, with wide short sleeves, and it was not belted. In early Christian images, the Christ and the Apostles wear the *pallium* and dalmatic.

The tunics were decorated with characteristic purple stripes called *clavi* on either side, from neck to hem. Their width was dictated by the status of the wearer: the wider the stripe, the more important the wearer. These stripes changed from simple bands to more decorative ones. Eventually, the two *clavi* became a single band down the centre front. Decorative roundels and squares were added, and hems were edged with decorative bands. This ornamentation was used on other garments as well. The toga had always had a purple edge; now the pallium, the *chlamys* and the dalmatic were decorated too.

The Byzantine Empress Theodora, 6th century.

(background image) Christian women and boy, 4th–6th century.

Textiles became richer, heavier and stiffer, and were encrusted with jewels and gold. This was a characteristic element of Byzantine court dress. The Byzantine silks were controlled by strict regulations as to who could use them. Certain types of silks and certain garments were reserved for the imperial family. The Byzantine fabrics had repeating patterns, not seen before, of stylized animal designs. A demand for these precious silks grew in the West after accounts were received from embassies about the magnificence of the Byzantine court. Some of these silks can still be found in the church treasuries of western Europe.

While in Byzantium, Roman dress was transformed into a stiff form, which hid the shape of the body. In the west, Germanic influences changed it in a different direction. On Roman monuments, such as Trajan's Column, Germanic men are in short-sleeved tunics and leggings, which cover the whole leg and are bound around the ankle. Their cloaks appear on the relief as a square cloth fastened on the right shoulder with a brooch, or as a cloak pulled over the head like a poncho or with a hood like a *paenula*. The Roman *tunica* had always been without sleeves or with short sleeves that never reached below the elbow. Long sleeves and the Barbarian fashion for leggings became more popular in men's dress.

The Germans in their turn were influenced by Roman and Byzantine dress. The Frankish kings wore the Byzantine tunics, but kept their leggings under them. There were many marriage alliances between Byzantium and the West to bring about change, among them the marriage of Princess Theophano with the Holy Roman Emperor Otto II (ruled 973–83).

In the North, the materials remained homespun wool or linen. Silks were worn only by the élite, and came mainly as gifts from the Byzantine court or as booty. Cotton was still quite rare, and amazement was caused by the cotton tent sent to Charlemagne (742–814) by Haroun-al-Raschid (?764–809). The quality of local materials must have been quite good, though, and export was already extensive.

Byzantine empresses, 6th–10th century (top left); Frankish king and clergy, 8th century (top right); Crusader, knight and soldiers, 11th century (bottom).

EARLY CHRISTIAN

CHRISTIANS

• 4TH–6TH CENTURY

In the third century AD, a new garment appeared, worn, at first, only by men. It was a T-shaped tunic with wide sleeves called a dalmatic: it was normal clothing in Dalmatia and for many Asiatic peoples. When laid out flat, it was cross-shaped, with a horizontal slit in the centre for the head; the cross was folded in half and sewn together along the sides to form a body and sleeves. It was like the Roman *tunica* but wider, with short wide sleeves. The dalmatic was decorated with *clavi*, red or purple bands down both sides, back and front; sometimes two bands of the same colour decorated the sleeves as well. Made of wool, linen or cotton, the dalmatic was worn without a belt. Men wore it to below the knee, sometimes showing an under-tunic.

As can be seen in fourth-century images, the dalmatic in combination with the pallium was the distinctive garment of the early Christians, worn by the figure in the middle. The figure on the left is wearing a different kind of *tunica*. It has fitted sleeves and has both *clavi* and decorative roundels, which would have been embroidered. The woman on the right has her tunic over an under-tunic with *clavi*. Repeating patterns were not seen in this region before the appearance of Byzantine fabrics, and these complicated patterns were almost always woven in silk.

CHRISTIAN WOMEN AND BOY
• 4TH–6TH CENTURY

In the fourth century, the T-shape of the dalmatic was modified. The sides of the tunic slanted diagonally from the armhole to the hem. The square sleeves were also cut on the slant. The clavi became more elaborate, often embroidered and with decorative edges. Tapestry weaving, embroidery and gold brocade developed during the late Empire, and decorative roundels and squares appeared at the shoulders and knees. Tunics were now girdled at the waist. An undergarment with fitted sleeves was worn. Sometimes, the sleeves showed under the wider sleeve of the dalmatic, and they often had decorative wristbands. Roman mantles and cloaks continued to be used.

Women covered their heads with a veil, and these were of various colours and fabrics. The quality and size of the textiles indicated the status of the wearer. Wealthy women wore them long and often richly decorated; the lower classes wore them only just long enough to cover the shoulders.

THE BYZANTINE EMPEROR JUSTINIAN AND THE EMPRESS THEODORA

• 6TH CENTURY

Based on the mosaics at San Vitale in Ravenna, 547, imperial dress here is slightly different colours. The Emperor Justinian has a semi-circular purple cloak fastened with a gem-studded brooch. He wears this over a long-sleeved knee-length white tunic with gold embroidered bands and roundels. The tunic is slit up the sides. On his cloak he has a *tablion*, which is like a badge, in cloth-of-gold with birds in circles. He has purple hose and shoes. The crown is a band that slopes outwards to the upper edge. It is decorated with gems and pearls.

The Empress Theodora wears a long version of his tunic with the hem and cuffs covered in rich gold, red and green. Her semi-circular purple cloak has the Three Magi embroidered along its hem. Empresses are not known to have worn the *tablion* before the eighth century. She has the jewelled collar of empresses called the *superhumeral*. The crown is made of gold, with gems and pearls. Strings of pearls drop down each side of her face ending in pear-shaped pearls.

BYZANTINE EMPRESSES

• 6TH–10TH CENTURY

The figure on the right is wearing almost the same as the Empress Theodora, without the heavy *superhumeral*. The empress beside her is in imperial dress of the tenth and eleventh centuries. The tunic now has a narrower line than previously. Over the tunic is a long ornamented band. This is a further development from the toga. The overlarge toga had for the sake of convenience been folded lengthways two or three times along its border. By the late fourth century, the superfluous layers underneath that border had been removed, with the remaining edge now forming a long scarf. Around her neck the empress still wears the jewelled collar.

On her elaborately padded and rolled hair is a crown: from around the ninth century, the band was made up of different linked pieces with an arch attached from front to back. A cross was added to the front.

EARLY CHRISTIAN

FRANKISH KING AND HIS COURT

• 8TH CENTURY

Frankish women's dress consisted of a floor-length under-tunic with long fitted sleeves worn over a linen shirt, which served as a house or work dress. Over this was a wider shorter tunic with short sleeves. A mantle was worn over all. Only unmarried girls wore their hair uncovered. Circular brooches, often made of gold and decorated with stones and enamel work, were used to secure the mantle. Men wore a linen shirt and drawers under a knee-length tunic, and boots or shoes.

Court dress differed from everyday dress in the richness of the materials. The embroidered and brocaded borders are evidence of Byzantine influence, and the silks used would have been imported from Byzantium. Charlemagne, who is said to have worn simple Frankish dress, did on certain occasions wear a tunic of cloth-of-gold, jewelled shoes and a mantle with a gold brooch.

On the table is the crown, made in the tenth century for Otto the Great (912–73) but known as the crown of Charlemagne. It is now in the treasury of the Hofburg in Vienna.

FRANKISH KING AND HIS COURT

• 9TH CENTURY

Copied from a miniature in the Codex Aureus of St Emmeram, 870, in the Munich State Library. Charles the Bald (823–77) seems to have been much taken with Byzantine dress when he went to Italy, and the chronicles of the Fulda monastery record in 876 that 'when he returned to Gaul, he took on the strange newfangled fashions. Dressed in a girdled dalmatic, which reached to the feet, his head covered in a silk bonnet with a diadem over it. This is how he appeared at church. The King despised old Frankish customs and now preferred Greek splendour.'

Charles the Bald liked to ring the changes, and it is said that he opened the Synod of Pontion in Frankish dress and closed it in a Greek gown. In miniatures, Charles the Bald still appears in Frankish dress, with a short tunic, hose and bindings.

It was especially the leggings that distinguished the Franks from the Mediterranean peoples. The legs and feet were covered in long hose, sometimes leaving the toes free. Boothose were often worn over this, which were then bound with leather thongs. A rectangular mantle was fastened with a brooch on the right shoulder. The shoes were pointed. Men were generally clean shaven at this date, though they sometimes had a moustache; the hair was worn short.

FRANKISH KING, SOLDIER AND CLERGY

• 8TH CENTURY

The soldier is dressed in a manner similar to the lifeguard of Charles the Bald as illustrated in a Bible dedicated to him. His bell-shaped iron helmet slants from the middle of the forehead to over the ears, its broad brim protecting the nape of the neck. On top is a red crest, which is perhaps made of copper. His armour is reminiscent of Roman armour, and is strengthened with leather and metal plates. His legwear follows the Frankish fashion of leggings bound around the leg with cross-gartered bands, leaving the toes uncovered.

Ecclesiastical dress, like secular dress, was based on a mixture of Byzantine and Roman dress. By the sixth century, when gentlemen had replaced the toga and *tunica* with the paenula and dalmatic, bishops wore these with the *pallium*. The Byzantine *pallium* had become stylized even further into a T-shape resting on the shoulders. The *paenula* became the chasuble. The priest on the left is dressed in a tent-like chasuble with a *pallium* over it. Under the chasuble is the alb, which is a white tunic. Deacons, like the priest on the right, wore the dalmatic with *clavi* over the alb.

CRUSADER KNIGHT AND SOLDIERS

• 11TH CENTURY

The knight and his men are not in full battle dress. The knight would have worn mail gloves and probably mail protection on his legs. Under the coat of mail, called a hauberk, he would have worn a padded garment, either quilted or of leather with metal plates. His hauberk is slit front and back to make riding easier. His helmet is conical, with a nose-piece called a nasal, and a neck-guard. His shield is kite-shaped and would have been made of wood covered with leather, its border and central boss reinforced with metal.

The soldier behind him is wearing a quilted garment, maybe instead of the coat of mail; or it is perhaps the tunic worn under the hauberk. He is carrying a lance with pennon. The soldier in the rear is wearing the mail coif without the helmet. It was usually the men of superior rank who wore a suit of mail. The Germanic coloured hose held up by cross-garters are worn by two of the men.

Asia and the Far East

Calcutta, Zaytoun, Mosul and Damascus conjure up the names of fabrics from the East – calico, satin, muslin and damask. While linen and wool were developed early on in the West, silk and cotton were very much the products of the East.

The silk industry probably originated in China during the third millennium BC. Production methods were strictly guarded until the first millennium BC, when silk was taken to India, central Asia, and Persia. India was soon producing its own raw silk and by the second century AD was shipping it to Persia. Japan also developed its own sericulture.

Around the first century AD, nomadic tribes invaded India from the north through Afghanistan, bringing with them woollen clothes. This led to the production of fine woollen textiles in north-western India.

Japanese Samurai. *second half of the 19th century.*

During the eighth and ninth centuries, Chinese silk production began to grow rapidly, and a boom trade soon followed. Textiles from China were taken across Asia by way of the various trade routes. Non-Chinese merchants dominated the foreign trade. Large Arab trading communities exised in southern China, and the Koreans traded on the northern coast. Central Asian and Persian merchants ran the overland trade.

The ancient Silk Road was actually a network of routes running from China through central Asia to Europe. At its peak, luxury goods including silk, lacquer, gems and spices were carried on these roads to the West, and fine muslins, woollens, carved ivories, glass, porphyry and alabaster came to China from India and Europe. It was a highway of culture as well as of commerce. Indian pilgrims introduced Buddhism into China, which China in turn took to Japan in the sixth century.

The 4000-mile Silk Road started in Siam and followed the Great Wall of China to the north-west, ran around the Takla Makan Desert, climbed the Pamir mountains, crossed Afghanistan – where Balkh became the centre of the trade routes – then went north to Bokhara and Samarkand, and west through Persia to the Mediterranean. Few travelled the entire road; instead, goods were passed along the route by merchants acting as middlemen. Oases grew into important centres of commerce.

There were probably Eastern trade links with the Levant as early as the second millennium BC, and these were later extended to the Mediterranean. At the height of the Roman Empire, the overland trade joined the cultures of Europe, north Africa, the Middle East, China and India.

Cotton came to the West by a different route. Traders brought cottons and other textiles from India to the Persian Gulf, and then via Egypt across the Mediterranean.

Persia was central to the silk trade between East and West and may have had its own sericulture by the third century. Syria, Egypt, Greece and Rome developed silk-weaving

industries, too. Even though they received raw silk from the East, the Romans usually unpicked the Chinese fabrics and re-wove them.

Constantinople obtained its raw silk from China either by land through Persia or by sea from Persian merchants. In the mid-sixth century, it managed to break the Persian monopoly by having silk worms smuggled out of China to Constantinople, and was thus able to establish its own silk industry.

The Silk Road had been there for over a thousand years by the time Marco Polo travelled it in the thirteenth century, but during much of that time it had been virtually impassable due to nomadic raids and wars. In the thirteenth and fourteenth centuries, the route was revived under the Mongols. Some of the roads were improved, and arrangements were made for the protection of merchants and other travellers. In China, the Mongols encouraged trade by getting rid of trade controls.

China's overland trade with the Middle East and Europe was still handled mainly by non-Chinese, and there was little direct contact between Europe and China. The Chinese carried on trade for centuries with other Asian countries such as Korea, Japan, Vietnam and Burma, and between those countries there was close cultural contact. There was also some exchange of culture and learning between the Muslim world and China, especially in matters of science.

As a result of the Mongol advance into eastern Europe, the West became aware of China, far more so than China seemed to be of the West. Franciscan missionaries were sent to the court of the Grand Khan, and their letters brought first-hand information on China to medieval Europe. But the missionaries made little impact on Chinese civilization, which remained relatively unchanged.

Over the centuries, trade switched between overland routes and sea routes, depending on the economic and political situation. The changes affected the prosperity of the cities and towns along the various routes. Aden was one of the main ports in the trade between the Mediterranean and the Indian Ocean. Merchants there had contacts all over north Africa, the Middle East and southern Europe. The trade in spices and silk was valuable, but the dangers met with on the way made it increasingly necessary for Europe to find other ways of reaching the East. In 1498, Vasco da Gama sailed around the coast of Africa and into the Indian Ocean; the Silk Road quickly lost out to the new sea route to India and the Far East.

The Silk Road was never abandoned completely, however. The Kashmir shawl, which caught the imagination of the Europeans at the end of the eighteenth century, was transported along the overland routes via Kabul, Novgorod and Constantinople to Europe, as well as being shipped by the East India Company from Surat and Calcutta to London. The designs on the shawls reflected the influence of places along the ancient trade routes, the typical pine motif showing both Persian and classical European elements.

Kirghiz woman, second half of 19th century (top left); Burmese women of Myanmar, 1886 (top right); Thai actor (bottom).

ASIA AND THE FAR EAST

CENTRAL ASIAN MEN AND WOMEN

• SECOND HALF OF 19TH CENTURY

The men may be wandering mendicant dervishes. They wear embroidered felt hats with fringes of horsehair. The man on the left has several layers of patched and embroidered coats held together with a wide decorative girdle.

Dress was based on the same garments all over central Asia but differed greatly in the details according to whether the wearer led a sedentary or a nomadic life, and also to which ethnic group and religion he belonged, and his status. The basic fabrics in sedentary dress were cotton and silk, whereas in nomadic dress it was mainly wool or hair.

Generally, both women and men wore baggy drawstring trousers that tapered at the ankle. Women wore a tunic known as a *kurta* over this. Unlike country women, urban women wore a veil. These could vary from fine silk to the thick horsehair ones of Turkoman women. On their feet they wore boots, the more expensive ones being decorated with embroidery. Turkoman women had much red woven and embroidered onto their clothes, and their bodices and headdresses were hung with coins, metal disks and jewellery.

MAN FROM KHIVA, EMIR OF BOKHARA, TEKKE TURKOMAN, GIRL FROM SAMARKAND AND MAN FROM BOKHARA

• SECOND HALF OF 19TH CENTURY

Headwear could identify the region the wearer came from. Turkomans, on the whole, wore large shaggy sheepskin hats, whereas the Kazakh wore fur ones and the Kirghiz felt ones. The man on the left is from Khiva, which was a vassal state of Russia. He has either a sheepskin or a fur hat. Over his trousers and shirt he could wear a waistcoat and a variety of overcoats, ranging from the thin long-sleeved *khalat* to the padded and quilted *chapan*. The *postin* could be of fur or sheepskin embroidered on the outside, or of silk with a lambskin lining as here.

The seated emir of Bokhara may be wearing a brocade *khalat*, which is edged with an embroidered or woven patterned border. Several coats were worn over each other. Honoured guests were presented by the emir with a silk *khalat*, which was also given as a reward for good service. The emir's turban is probably made of silk, which was worn only by the aristocracy.

The Tekke Turkoman at the back in the middle has his coat open to reveal a shirt and waistcoat. A girdle is worn around the waist. Made of a square of cotton, this could serve as a pouch or be spread out for use as a prayer mat. The girl is in her *kurta*. Unmarried girls had many small plaits, whereas married women had only two.

CHUKCHI, BURYAT AND KHANT MEN AND WOMEN

• SECOND HALF OF 19TH CENTURY

The people in this illustration are from regions as distant from each other as arctic Siberia and northern Mongolia. They are in consequence very different. The Chukchi come from the far north-east, where they are divided into inland and coastal groups. The inland groups live on the tundras herding reindeer, whereas the coastal groups hunt and fish. The Buryat are the most northern of the Mongol peoples and live south and west of Lake Baikal. They are nomadic, with a stock of cattle, sheep, goats, horses and some camels. The Khant, who used to be known as the Ostyak, live in swamp and forest country around the Ob river, where they hunt and fish.

The Chukchi woman on the left has tattoos on her face and arms. She wears a sealskin tunic, and shirt and breeches. The seated Buryat has a gown of Chinese silk. His cap has a jewelled band, and silk bands of hair hang down from it. The Khant women on the right have covered their hair with kerchiefs and wear large heavy coats: one is for everyday wear, the other is very decorated and a part of festive dress.

SIBERIAN WOMAN FROM TOMSK, AND KIRGHIZ MAN AND WOMAN

• SECOND HALF OF 19TH CENTURY

The Kirghiz were nomadic shepherds of Mongol origin. They wore baggy drawstring trousers with a shirt. Over this, coats of different varieties were worn. The woman in the middle has a coat over her tunic. She is in festive dress, with a curious tall headdress. The front of her bodice is covered with jewellery and coins. Around her waist is a girdle made from a twisted length of patterned fabric.

The man on the right has a coat that crosses over in the front and is probably embroidered; it is lined with fur. He has a tall pointed hat made of felt and lined with fur. The woman on the left is from Tomsk. She is in a wide tunic with a coat over it. Both the coat and the tunic have been embroidered with gold thread. The coat is lined with sheepskin. She has wrapped a large kerchief around her head and covered it with a fabric-covered hat with a fur brim.

ASIA AND THE FAR EAST

WOMAN, LIFEGUARD AND MARAJA OF KASHMIR

• SECOND HALF OF 19TH CENTURY

These figures are based on photographs. The woman's garments would have been made of fine silks and cottons and are embroidered with delicate motifs along the edges. She wears a jewelled headdress and over it a fine silk veil edged with embroidery. Jewels were much worn and were thought to contain magic. Nose-rings were an Islamic fashion. The lifeguard at the back has a large headdress that may be made of tough yak wool. He has a close-fitting tunic and trousers. The sash around his waist possibly denotes his rank.

The illustration of the maharaja is after a photograph by John Burke of 1870–90. The maharaja is in typical Rajasthani court dress, which includes the close-fitting tunic and the breeches of a warrior. Around his neck is a magnificent necklace. An elaborate sash, the *patka*, is tied around the waist as a mark of dignity. His outer gown is short sleeved in the photograph on which this illustration is based. It has magnificent embroidered borders and is lined with fur. He holds an ornate sword, and a dagger is tucked into his sash. The turban is decorated with turban jewels and feathers. His order, seen more clearly in the original photograph, is the Most Exalted Star of India.

TIBETAN WOMEN AND MEN

• SECOND HALF OF 19TH CENTURY

Tibetans are followers of Buddhism, which came from India in the seventh century, and with this they mixed local beliefs. On the high plains of Tibet it can be bitterly cold, and several layers of wool and sheepskin were necessary. The coat, or *chupa*, would often be of sheepskin or cotton sateen, worn with the fur inside. The woman's coat was usually more decorated and reached almost to the floor. A thinner outer coat would sometimes be put on over this. These coats crossed over at the front, and the space formed on the chest could be used for storing necessary items. Bulky cummerbunds around the waist were also used as pouches, and they held the layers of coats together. When the temperature rose, a part of the coat could be taken off and left hanging down the back; often this was a sleeve.

Both the men and the women in the illustration wear silver jewellery, and coral and turquoise stones in their hair and on their person. Men had long hair that could be pinned to the top of their heads or left long. The man on the right holds a rosary, which had to consist of 108 beads, a sacred Buddhist number. The pouch on his cummerbund is a tinder and flint pouch.

AFGHAN GENTLEMEN AND SERVANT

• SECOND HALF OF 19TH CENTURY

The man on the left has a striped coat that shows its central Asian origin. It has extra-long sleeves that can be pulled down over the hands. He wears it over pyjamas and several layers of garments that cross over at the front. The man at the back has a coat that fastens with a special loop and two buttons. He wears it over trousers and a tunic with a wide pleated skirt. The man on the right has a tunic woven or embroidered with gold to match part of his turban. Over his undergarments he wears a *choga*, a long formal coat that has been embroidered at the bottom corners. It fastens with two buttons, like the servant's coat.

Turbans were made of long lengths of fabric, some over 20 ft (6 m.). They were wound in a variety of shapes and would identify where the wearer came from. The two seated men have wound two contrasting lengths together.

THREE AFGHAN MEN FROM THE KHYBER PASS

• SECOND HALF OF 19TH CENTURY

The man on the left wears a three-quarter-length outer coat with lapels and slits up the sides, probably made of a woollen cloth woven locally. He has a sash bound around his waist. Over his shoulder is draped a shawl that matches his coat. He wears a white tunic and trousers underneath, and a skullcap on his head. The man in the middle has a longer coat over his white tunic and trousers. He too has a shawl draped around him. The man on the right has a similar tunic and trousers covered with a sheepskin coat with the fur worn on the inside. These coats were often beautifully embroidered.

Two of the men wear turbans, which were multi-functional: they protected the wearer from the sun; the hanging tail end could be held in front of the face against sand and dust; and it could be used as a handkerchief or knotted into a purse.

ASIA AND THE FAR EAST

PARSEES OF BOMBAY AND SINGAPORE

• SECOND HALF OF 19TH CENTURY

Parsees are descended from Persian Zoroastrians who from around the eighth century emigrated to India. The largest community lives in and around Bombay. The seated woman wears a sari over her petticoat and blouse. The sari could be of wool or silk, depending on the climate. The length and the way of draping it varied, but in essence it was the same garment in every region. It was always a length of cloth wound around as a skirt, and draped across the top half and over the shoulder.

The woman in the background is a widow and wears a colourless sari. The woman on the right has a highly patterned sari that has been wound around with the end hanging down the front. She wears it with a striped jacket. The man has a long fitted coat, or *achkan*, which buttons from collar to waist and is left open down to the hem. He wears it over plain white trousers. His tall hat is bound with cloth.

RAJPUT RULER AND HIS SON, RAJASTHANI WOMAN AND HINDU WOMAN

• SECOND HALF OF 19TH CENTURY

The ruler is in the close-fitting coat and breeches of the warrior. A round-shaped piece fills the gap on his chest. The coat is long and made of a richly decorated material. He wears a *patka* around his waist. The ornate necklace around his neck displays nine gems, representing the nine planets. The circular shield, sword and dagger are part of ceremonial Rajput dress. There should be five weapons: the spear and the small throwing-knife, hidden in the back of the coat, are missing. The turban is decorated with jewels and has a silk band wound around it. His slippers are embroidered with coloured and gold threads.

The boy is dressed in a miniature version of the dress of his father. The woman on the right is from Rajasthan. Her dress consists of several garments: a full pleated skirt, a half-sleeved bodice, trousers and a length of material that is passed over the head and either tucked into the bodice or the skirt. This last article is sometimes pleated at the front like a sari. Jewellery covers her head, neck, arms and ankles. The Hindu woman at the back is in a sari girdled at the waist.

KANDYAN DANCERS OF CEYLON

• 1880

Kandyan dancing combines song and dance. The song does not interpret the dance in any way and is purely a musical accompaniment. Traditionally, it was performed as a religious ritual, but it became secularized. To the sound of the drums, a team of five or six men moved in unison using intricate symbolic gestures.

The costume is based on the ceremonial regalia of a mythical king. The headdress, a sacred object, consists of a tiara that should have seven silver points surrounding the wooden crown in rays. A long embroidered ribbon falls from the top down the back. The ears are covered by ornately shaped pieces. The shoulders are covered with metal bands. Eight sets of strands of coloured beads are interlaced around the the torso, fanning out from a central point, with ivory or horn and silver studs marking the points where the strands connect. The lower half of the body is covered by three layers of pleated cloth. A large belt decorated with silver studs encircles the waist, with a long shaped piece hanging down the front to the knees.

SINGHALESE GENTLEMAN AND LADIES

• 1880

The man wears a white cotton shirt and trousers with a frilled hem. A silk cloth like a sarong, called a *tuppotti*, is wrapped around and bound by an ornate belt. The quantity and size of the cloth varied according to the class of the wearer, with the superior classes wearing several layers of longer *tuppotti*. Above this is a quilted silk jacket with short puffed sleeves. His elaborate four-cornered hat indicates that he is the governor of a province. He is in full dress, and his hat is of scarlet cloth embroidered with gold. The brim has a tooth-shaped edge and on the top is a stiff ornament known as the *boralé*.

The women have blouses with elbow-length puff sleeves. The seated woman has a blouse decorated with lace. They have both wrapped full-length silk sarongs around them. A second length of silk is pleated and draped from one shoulder, and bound by a girdle at the waist. Both men and women wear jewellery: bracelets, necklaces, rings and earrings. The best gold jewellery was said to come from Kandy.

ASIA AND THE FAR EAST

BURMESE WOMEN OF MYANMAR

• 1886

The women wear long wrapped sarongs that trail along the ground. They are made of colourful silks with horizontal patterned bands or with a floral pattern. Above the sarong they wear a cloth covering the upper torso. Over this they have fitted jackets. The woman sitting at the front has a kind of tunic. The woman on the left has draped a shawl over her right shoulder. They all have their hair pinned up close to the head. The women at the front and on the left have decorated their hair with flowers.

There was a long tradition of goldsmiths' work in Burma, and the jewellery shows influences from both China and India. Rubies and sapphires from Burma were always highly prized because of their wonderful colours. The women here do not appear to be wearing gems, but they have earrings, rings and necklaces. The lady in front has pinned her necklaces to her tunic.

BURMESE MAN AND WOMEN OF MYANMAR

• 1886

The man on the left and the woman in front are textile workers. The man is standing by a loom and the woman is at a spinning-wheel. They are described as weavers of *pu cho*, the name for a man's sarong. In earlier times, the Burmese did not wear silk as it involved killing an animal, which as devout Buddhists they could not do. However, in the eighteenth and nineteenth centuries, the Burmese silks were well known.

The man has a short white jacket fastened with a loop and button, and a checked sarong. The man's sarong was sewn together along one side, making it into a tubular garment. It was then gathered at the front and hitched in, and worn long or short. On his head is a small turban. The woman at the front is in a striped sarong and a tunic decorated with spots. Her hair is pinned up and decorated with flowers. The lady at the back is from Ava, which from the fourteenth to the nineteenth century was periodically the capital of Burma. She has a long dark coat over her sarong. Her hair is pinned up with gold pins. She has gold embroidered slippers.

THAI ACTORS AND ACTRESSES

• SECOND HALF OF 19TH CENTURY

Khon is one of the oldest forms of theatre in Thailand. Although mainly performed at court, the plays were sometimes put on in the open air for the people. Episodes from the *Ramayana* were used as the basis of this dance drama. The most popular episodes concerned the deeds of the monkey kings Hanuman and Sukhrip, and scenes with Rama and Sita and involving the evil Ravana, who in Thailand is called Thosakan. The actors conveyed the action through gestures and mime. A singer accompanied by musicians sang the text. There were no actresses apart from those playing the principal female roles.

The actor in the middle is Phra Ram (Rama) and the actress on the right is Nang Sida (Sita). The masked figure on the left is Thosakan, the devil king born with ten heads. The masks are made of papier-mâché covered with gold paint, with holes for the eyes but not for the mouth. The ear decorations and headdresses are of leather and wood, inset with pieces of mirror-glass and glass.

KING RAMA V OF SIAM WITH THE QUEEN AND CHILD, AND A BHUDDIST MONK

• SECOND HALF OF 19TH CENTURY

This represents of King Rama V on his Coronation Day in 1873. He has a short tunic with a type of sarong, both of a rich silk with a deep gold-embroidered hem. Ornate gold pieces encrusted with gems are laid over the top. The king's tiered crown is known as the Great Crown of Victory; on his feet are special slippers turned up at the front and in his lap is the ceremonial sword.

The queen wears a shawl, or *pha sabai*, draped around the upper body and over one shoulder. It is of Thai silk, either embroidered or with a woven pattern. Her blouse under the *sabai* has long sleeves and a standing collar, and opens down the front with five buttons. The wrapped skirt is made of gold brocade, and is pleated in front and held by a belt. The young prince has a topknot. Much care was taken over this single lock, and the hair-cutting ceremony was an important event, celebrating the beginning of manhood.

ASIA AND THE FAR EAST

MEN AND WOMEN FROM SUMATRA AND SULAWESI

• SECOND HALF OF 19TH CENTURY

The two girls and the man at the left are Minangkabau, from the largest ethnic group in Sumatra. Traditionally, their heredity went through the female line. Their ceremonial clothes were woven in gold and silver cloth, the finest woven with 24-carat-gold thread. The motifs symbolized the hierarchical order in their society. They are a mainly Muslim people, and the patterns are therefore mostly floral and geometric. *Minang kabau* means 'victorious water buffalo', and the headdresses of the women were folded to look like the horns of the water buffalo.

The men's ceremonial garments and headdresses were also folded in a particular way. The Batak of northern Sumatra wore their own cloths in dark colours with stripes and checks in *ikat*. They were worn as wrapped sarongs and draped around their shoulders. The man in the middle has a turban-like headdress decorated with green leaves. The man from Sulawesi on the right has a rich cloth around his lower half with a striking red and white zigzag pattern along the open sides.

REGENT OF CIREBON IN JAVA WITH HIS SERVANT, AND MAN FROM THE ISLAND OF NIAS

• SECOND HALF OF 19TH CENTURY

The traditional dress of Malaysia and Indonesia is the sarong and *kebaya*, a long-sleeved jacket usually made of cotton. There are variations on the jacket and sarong which are cut in different ways and have different names. The *kebaya* is made of rectangles cut with curved seams to the side to give a fitted bodice and flared skirt. The sarong, which is sewn down the side, is secured at the waist with a cotton girdle. Sometimes a stole, or *selendang*, is worn over the shoulder.

Cirebon in Java was a prosperous Muslim city with a flourishing textile industry. The regent wears batik-patterned trousers and sarong, with a jacket and waistcoat over his shirt. Java is the home of batik production. The man at the front has a jacket and shirt over a sarong. He has a flat round cap on top of his turban. The man from Nias, on the right, has the mitre-shaped headdress worn at ritual celebrations.

MEN AND WOMEN FROM ANNAM

• SECOND HALF OF 19TH CENTURY

Vietnam was divided into three regions: Tonkin in the north, Annam in the centre and Cochinchina in the south. The traditional royal capital of Hue was in Annam. Before French colonial rule in the nineteenth century, the administration more or less followed the Chinese model. The palace in Hue was modelled on the Manchu palace in Peking. The bureaucracy was run by a hierarchy of mandarins under an absolute monarch.

The seated man is dressed in a coat of transparent black gauze with a standing collar that crosses over the front and fastens with small gold buttons. Under this outer coat would be a white jacket, shirt and very loose cotton trousers. He wears a black turban, and slippers decorated with red and white zigzags. The women wear jackets closed right up to the neck, often covered with a flowing cotton coat reaching almost to the ankles. Like the men, the women wear wide thin cotton trousers. The round hat by the knees of the seated woman is a palm-leaf hat. Women twisted a black cloth around the long single braid and wound this about the head. The Annamese blackened their teeth.

WOMEN AND MEN OF TONKIN

• SECOND HALF OF 19TH CENTURY

The northern region, Tonkin, had Hanoi as its urban centre. The most obvious difference between the two regions was in the headdresses. Tonkinese women wore enormous hats around 2½ to 3 feet (76 cm to 90 cm) in diameter. They were flat on top and made of leaves. There was a small round inner support on which this large shape rested. Ties were made of black crêpe or of silk rope, with large tassels that sometimes reached to the ground.

While the Annamese wore mostly black and white, the Tonkinese were dressed in a various reddish browns. Women usually wore loose cinnamon-coloured knee-length jackets, skirts or very loose, thin, black trousers, and wooden sandals. Both men and women who could afford to do so wore gold and other valuable ornaments, such as necklaces, bracelets and earrings. Soldiers wore blue, and had conical hats with brass tops and imperial yellow leggings.

ASIA AND THE FAR EAST

CHINESE MAN FROM HOKIEN AND CHINESE MERCHANT FROM PENANG

• SECOND HALF OF 19TH CENTURY

The man on the left is in standard Chinese dress: he wears a cotton jacket that fastens in front and trousers. Some went barefoot, like this man, but others had black cotton shoes with quilted soles. While the lower classes wore cotton and woollen clothing, the upper classes wore satin, damask and silk.

The long mandarin gown of the seated man is cut in the same way as the cotton jacket, but it has a long skirt. This man's dress is that of an official within the Chinese bureaucracy. In the second half of the nineteenth century, the Chinese government awarded various wealthy men a place in the hierarchy in order to secure financial donations from them. His outer gown, called a *pu fu*, is decorated front and back with a square patch that indicates his rank. A pair of trousers, a shirt and a waistcoat are worn under the two gowns. When on official business, he would have had an elaborately patterned robe under his gown, known as a dragon robe. He wears a beaded necklace around his neck with four short strands hanging from it, which is part of his insignia. His boots are satin with thick white soles.

CHINESE MERCHANT FROM PENANG AND WOMAN FROM MACAO

• SECOND HALF OF 19TH CENTURY

The merchant appears much more formal than in the illustration above. He has a damask *pu fu* with official patches that he wears over a silk robe. The shoulder collar is detachable and is part of full dress, as is his hat. He wears a summer hat; winter hats had upturned brims. Summer hats were made of split cane and straw and were covered with silk gauze. The outside would be overlaid with fringes of red silk cord. On top was a round knob of coloured glass, semi-precious stone or metal, according to the status of the wearer. This dress was enormously expensive, and the cost would often prevent men who were entitled to from taking up their commission.

The woman is in a skirt and robe. The skirt is made of several alternating straight and pleated panels. She would have worn this over trousers or some kind of leggings, tied at the waist and ankles. Over this was a kind of chemise that reached to the hips. Next came the gown with wide sleeves that crossed the front and fastened on the right side; Chinese women never accentuated their waists with girdles or belts. Her feet are unbound and she wears normal-sized shoes.

JAPANESE SAMURAI

• SECOND HALF OF 19TH CENTURY

During the second half of the nineteenth century, a struggle went on to modernize Japan. The traditional life style of the *samurai* was to change radically during this transitional period. The *samurai* here have not yet adapted to that change. They wear wide trousers called *hakama*, put on over a kimono. Under these they would wear a loincloth and a thigh-length cotton garment shaped like the kimono. Next a girdle, or *obi*, is tied around the waist, made of heavy silk for formal dress and of a lighter silk or cotton for everyday dress. A little box is attached to the *obi* for storing necessary items. The cords of the box are held by two knobs, or *netsuke*, shaped into animals or portraits of gods. The outer garment is the *haori*. Thigh length, it hangs open and is held together by two silk cords. It is always dark in colour and decorated with five crests called the *mon*.

The man in the middle has a very formal gown, which should be worn over very long *hakama* and only when visiting the *shogun*. His white socks are of silk or cotton and made with a separate big toe. The sandals with a flat sole made of rice-straw or bamboo are called *zori*. Men shaved their foreheads, and the hair would be laid on the top of the head in a tail. *Samurai* always carried a long and a short sword.

JAPANESE WOMEN

• SECOND HALF OF 19TH CENTURY

The kimono is made of seven parts, with a seam at the centre back. It is stitched together with large stitches so that it is easily taken apart for cleaning. The undergarments consist of a wrapped skirt and a chemise, usually coloured and made of cotton, wool or silk. The women's kimono is similar to the men's, but the collar and sleeves are longer and wider. The colour and design of the kimono depend on the season and the occasion on which it is worn. The difference between the kimono worn by the rich and by the poor is in the quality of the textile. The *obi* is often the most valuable item and can be made of rich brocade. It can be up to 5 feet (1.5 m.) in length. A silk or cotton girdle is worn under the *obi* to keep the kimono in place.

The woman with the parasol and the nanny are unmarried; married women shaved their eyebrows and blackened their teeth. The pins and comb, made of bone or tortoiseshell, in the hair of the lady on the right show that she is married. Parasols were imported from the Philippines in the sixteenth century. The woman on the right has the high wooden sandals called *geta*.

The Ottoman Empire

The Ottoman Empire began with a Turkoman nomadic tribe entering Anatolia in the eleventh century. At first, the men were fighters for the faith of Islam against the Byzantine state. However, a struggle for territory later involved battles with Islamic Mongols as well. The Ottoman Empire would vary greatly in size during those six centuries. At its peak it included the Balkans, parts of Hungary and Russia, the Middle East, parts of Arabia and north Africa as far west as Algeria. The Ottoman Empire lasted for six centuries and came to an end in 1924, when the republic of Turkey came into existence under Kemal Atatürk (president 1923–38).

The word Ottoman came from a prince of the Turkoman tribe called Osman (1259–1326). His descendants would become sultans in Constantinople. The great periods of expansion took place from the fourteenth to the sixteenth centuries, starting in western Anatolia, then moving into south-eastern Europe and eventually east into Iraq and Arabia, and west into north Africa.

Murad I (ruled 1359–89) introduced a system of vassal states to the Ottomans in Europe. He kept on local native rulers, who in return accepted his sovereignty. In accepting Ottoman rule, their way of life was preserved and their properties protected. It was a policy to which there was little local resistance, and the Ottomans ruled over the conquered regions without having to build up an administrative system or to keep any occupation forces. Conversion to Islam was not required at this time.

The Ottomans were influenced not only by the traditions of the nomadic Turkic empires of central Asia and Islam but also by the Christian Byzantine, Serbian and Bulgarian empires. During the fourteenth century, marriage alliances were formed between the Ottoman and Christian courts. Several sultans married Byzantine, Serbian and Bulgarian princesses. Christian courtiers and advisers came to the Ottoman court in their train, and the old nomadic ways at court were abandoned in favour of elaborate Byzantine hierarchies and ceremonials. This trend of westernization was reversed under Bajazet II (Sultan 1481–1512), when Muslim traditions and the use of the Turkish language were re-enforced.

Constantinople was eventually captured by the Ottomans in 1453. During the sixteenth century, under Selim I (ruled 1512–20) and his son Suleiman the Magnificent (ruled 1520–66), Ottoman power reached its peak, and its empire extended to Vienna. From this moment the Ottoman Empire started its long, slow decline.

Ottoman dress changed little over the centuries. Each region kept its own traditions and styles, and there was some variation in the fabrics, and in the colours and decorations, but the basic garments remained the same. This was true for both dress at

Turkish pasha, 17th and first half of 18th century.

(background image) Egyptian men and women, second half of 19th century.

Turkish sultan, sultana and dancer, 17th and first half of 18th century (top left); Dalmatian women, second half of 19th century (top right); Egyptian women and man, second half of 19th century (bottom).

court and in the street. The difference was always in the quality of the textiles or the number of garments worn, rather than in the shapes. Various influences determined what form the dress should take. From the Turks came the caftan and trousers; from the Byzantine peoples the silks, jewelled embroideries and cloths-of-gold. The Ottomans eagerly adopted these rich and colourful textiles, and by the sixteenth century sumptuary laws were introduced forbidding the wearing of certain materials and decorations except by the sultan and his court.

The Turks had been regarded in European eyes as a threat during their periods of expansion, but with peace they came to be seen as belonging to the exotic East. Trade brought the empire and Europe closer together, and Venice became an important centre for both.

Textiles came from all over the empire. The Ottomans benefited from the silk industry started up by the Byzantines. Bursa in north-western Turkey had been an important Byzantine silk-weaving centre, and it was a thriving silk-trading centre from the fourteenth century; from the fifteenth century, it was exporting its velvets and silks to both Europe and Asia. The wool industry of Salonika in Greece provided the cloth for the uniforms of the janisseries. Embroiderers came from the Balkans, Hungary and Russia. Metal-thread embroidery was strictly controlled, and gold embroidery was reserved for imperial use.

From the mid-nineteenth century, a movement of Europeanization began throughout the empire, modernizing the old ways by substituting Western ideas and technology; but this was a slow process, and really only affected the élite and people in the urban areas of the empire.

THE OTTOMAN EMPIRE

TURKISH GENTLEMEN AND PASHA

• 17TH AND FIRST HALF OF 18TH CENTURY

The pasha was the highest official title of honour in the Ottoman Empire. It was always preceded by the man's name. The pasha in the illustration is in a silk brocade caftan fastened with buttons and tied around with a wide sash. Over this he has a short-sleeved gown that is fur lined and open down the front. On his head is a large turban wound around a high cap, and decorated with a jewel and feather aigret. He has a large jewel at his throat and a metalwork belt over his sash.

The man on the left has the wide baggy trousers that all the men wore. Over this he has a shirt, a short coat and a caftan with long hanging sleeves. It is closed with button and loop fastenings, and the front is hitched up into the waist sash. He has a shorter more rounded cap than the pasha, encircled by a small turban.

The man on the right is perhaps from north Africa. His gown overlaps at the front and closes at the side. It is tied with a sash. Over it he has an open gown. His turban is less structured and a different shape from those of the other men.

TURKISH SOLDIERS

• 17TH AND FIRST HALF OF 18TH CENTURY

The word janissery, or *yeniçeri*, means 'new soldier'. Janisseries were members of an élite corps in the Ottoman army from the late fourteenth century to 1826. Until the early eighteenth century, they were Christian converts to Islam from the Balkans.

The man with his back turned is in the uniform of a janissery. Made of coarse wool, his caftan is hitched up to show the breeches, which were perhaps rather baggier than shown here. On his belt he carries a powderhorn, and a sabretache and sword are suspended from his shoulder belt. His cap, topped by a large plume of blue and white feathers, identifies him as a janissery.

The janissery in the red cap may be from a different division, the colour signifying that he is Turkish by birth and a Muslim. The man on the left is an archer. His helmet is almost completely covered by a white turban. His caftan is hitched into the waist sash, revealing another caftan underneath. He wears boots and carries a bow-case on his right shoulder.

TURKISH NOBLEWOMAN, SULTAN AND SULTANA, AND DANCER

•17TH AND FIRST HALF OF 18TH CENTURY

The woman on the left is in outdoor dress. She has a caftan lined in a patterned silk. Normally she would wear a *feràce*, a large enveloping cloak that for ordinary women would be black, but for rich women or women from the court could be a light-coloured silk. Around her shoulders is a fringed scarf that goes over her high red cap and covers her lower face.

The sultana next to her wears baggy trousers called *salvar* and a chemise made of a fine material. Over this she wears a waistcoat called a *yelek*, the sleeves of which are visible. A long gown, or *anteri*, with hanging sleeves, is worn on top. This is bound around the waist by a long fringed scarf, or *kushak*. The *anteri* has probably been cut into three by making a slit at each side; all three parts have been tucked into the *kushak*. In her right hand she carries a fan, which was an important accessory. On her head is a cap made of rich materials, decorated with gold and silver ornaments and topped with an aigret. On her feet are embroidered slippers, or *çipship*.

TURKISH CAVALRYMEN

•17TH AND FIRST HALF OF 18TH CENTURY

The man on the left is in a woollen caftan with a wide flat collar and leather boots. A multi-coloured striped sash is tied around his waist. On his head is a bonnet with an upturned brim and a single feather in the front. A figure similar to this appears in sixteenth-century costume books. He carries a mace and a shield. The man with the fur hat at the back may be a stable boy; he too is represented in the costume books.

The man in the middle is in a magnificent gown that is patterned all over with a colourful design. It crosses over at the front and fastens at the side. A mace is tucked into his *kushak*. He wears boots and has a tall helmet beneath his turban. The man on the right is in a caftan that is buttoned to the waist, revealing a blue lining. He has a narrow sash, boots and a steel and brass helmet decorated with red feathers.

THE OTTOMAN EMPIRE

WOMAN AND MEN FROM THE OTTOMAN BALKANS

• SECOND HALF OF 19TH CENTURY

The woman is from Prizren in Kosovo. She is in indoor dress. Outside she would be covered in a large *feràce*. She wears pink *salvar* with a full-length chemise and an *anteri*, edged with gold braid, on top. This has been tied with a wide sash around the waist. A short jacket, with or without sleeves, would be worn, and she wears a caftan covered with gold embroidery and braid. On her head is a small cap edged with coins over a white scarf.

The man on the left is from Skodra in Albania. He has a short jacket with cord decoration along its edges that crosses over at the front and closes on the left side. He wears a caftan over it. The man with the white cap at the centre is an Albanian from Ioannina in north-western Greece. He wears a *fustanella*, the white skirt worn by both Greek and Albanian men. He has a western European shirt with two short jackets, one on top of the other. Over his shoulders he has draped a caftan. The sash around his waist also functions as a pouch. The man on the right is a Christian from Bulgaria, drawn from a photograph by Pascal Sébah. He is dressed for winter in an embroidered fur-lined coat over a cross-over coat. Beneath he has thick trousers, probably more than one pair, that have been bound up the legs.

WOMEN AND MEN FROM THE OTTOMAN BALKANS

• SECOND HALF OF 19TH CENTURY

The woman on the left is from the mountains north of Skodra. Her garments are of a felt-like woollen material decorated with braidwork, embroidery and appliqué in geometric patterns. She has on several layers over a stiff skirt. A decorated apron is worn over this both front and back. A long wide sash is worn around her hips and a girdle with metal clasps over this. She has a fringed shawl on her shoulder, and a kerchief over an elaborate headdress that has fringes attached at the back and coins along the front.

The man in the middle is from Edirne. He has a shirt under an indigo cross-over jacket that has been embroidered in black. He wears another indigo jacket over this, and his baggy trousers are also indigo. He wears a fez, which at this period was part of Turkish men's dress.

The woman on the right is from Saloniki. She is dressed for outdoors and is completely covered in a pale blue *feràce*. Her head is covered with heavy veiling.

DALMATIAN WOMAN AND MEN

• SECOND HALF OF 19TH CENTURY

Red, in eastern Europe, was believed to provide
protection against witches. The man in the middle has
a coat with red embroidery along the seams and top front
edges over his trousers and red waistcoat. Two wide sashes
are wrapped around his waist, the top one acting as a
pouch. Certain garments such as the sash and the woman's
apron were endowed with magical properties.

The girl on the left has a spectacular fringed apron, and it
is clear that this, with her headdress, is a special garment.
Underneath it all is the ancient dalmatic. Over this is a short
jacket edged with braids ending in small tassels. The outer
coat is sleeveless, and edged with red and gold. Her plaits
end with gold coins, a feature seen in central Asia too. The
socks are knitted with designs in geometric patterns.

DALMATIAN WOMEN

• SECOND HALF OF 19TH CENTURY

These women wear a different style of chemise: it is
gathered in at the neck and at the wrists. They wear it
with a linen skirt and a sleeved bodice. Over this, two wear a
sleeveless coat and an apron. The girl on the left has no sash
while two of them have. The edges of the coats have been
decorated with appliqué, embroidery and tassels.

The girl with her back turned is a back view of the figure in
the illustration above. The fringed veil, which has been
embroidered, is shown to be attached to the headdress. The
girl on the left has a headdress similar to that worn in Italy. It
is a folded cloth forming a flat-padded top, perhaps serving as
protection against the sun. The girl next to her has a simple
kerchief draped over her head, and the girl on the right has a
fez, or *tarboosh*, and a linen kerchief.

THE OTTOMAN EMPIRE

SYRIAN WOMAN AND MEN

• SECOND HALF OF 19TH CENTURY

The population of this region was ethnically diverse, and all three monotheistic religions were represented: Jewish, Christian and Muslim. The girl on the left is Armenian; the Armenians were usually Christian. Under her outer clothes she would have baggy trousers and a long chemise. Next comes the robe that is open down the front. It is bound by a long wide sash. She has a short jacket with hanging sleeves. On her head is a striped scarf. She has many bangles, bracelets and necklaces.

The man in the middle is a Druse, from the Middle Eastern religious sect. His headcloth is a square of tufted cotton large enough to be wound around his head and cover his face. It is worn over a skullcap and secured by a cord called an *agaal*.

The man on the right is from Damascus. His outer garment is the striped *qumbaz*. It opens down the front and fastens to one side, and was worn by men all over the Levant. A Western-style shirt collar can be seen at his neck. It was always the town dwellers who were the first to show Western influences. His baggy trousers underneath peep out from the bottom of his *qumbaz*. He has an embroidered jacket and waistcoat, and around his waist is a cummerbund. All of the men covered their heads, and most wore a kind of mantle when outside.

SYRIAN WOMAN AND MEN

• SECOND HALF OF 19TH CENTURY

The man on the left is a dervish, a member of the Sufi fraternity. Their rituals include recitation and dancing. The outer garment is a black caftan symbolizing the grave, while the tall camel-hair hat represents the headstone. The garments underneath are a wide pleated white robe and short jacket. When dancing, the black caftan is discarded. The head of the order wears a green scarf wound around his hat. The seated Syrian man is a farmer or peasant, a *fellah*. The many layers of his dress can be seen quite clearly here. He has various undergarments, baggy trousers and waistcoats under the outer striped *qumbaz*. His cap is bound around with a scarf.

The Druse woman has much gold jewellery around her wrists and neck. Various symbols of good luck and fertility would be attached to the necklace, such as crescents, frogs and salamanders. The 'hand of Fatima', a hand-shaped amulet, is another powerful symbol to protect against the evil eye. The man on the right is an Ottoman official, or *kavass*, from Damascus. His baggy trousers have Turkish silver and gold braiding around the hems. His short jacket has hanging sleeves that are split to allow his arms through. It is decorated with embroidery and cordwork, and is as seen in all the countries ruled by the Ottoman Empire. On his head, his fez with its long tassel is bound with a scarf.

LEBANESE MEN AND WOMAN

• SECOND HALF OF 19TH CENTURY

Lebanese Maronites belonged to a Christian sect. They were tough, martial, mountain people. Mainly because of their geographical isolation, they managed to maintain their religion and customs under the protection of France during the Ottoman period. The Maronite on the left wears baggy trousers and a jacket with a long cream mantle over it. His headcloth has striped borders. Various weapons are suspended from his girdle and shoulder strap.

The man from Zeibek in the middle is also heavily armed. He is part of the *bashi-bazoukd*, a troop that was mainly Kurdish. Several sashes and cummerbunds hold his weapons. His shins are protected by decorative leather greaves. His jacket, decorated with gold braids, has hanging sleeves that are split to allow his arms through. On his head is a turban of various materials wound around a tall cap with a fez on top.

The woman is a Lebanese Christian. She has a tasselled tarboosh on her head. She wears highly decorated baggy trousers with a chemise and an *anteri* worn open. The *anteri* is edged with gold embroidery and cordwork. She has a fringed sash around her waist.

SYRIAN MAN, DRUSE WOMAN AND BAGHDAD ARAB

• SECOND HALF OF 19TH CENTURY

The man on the left is a Syrian from Belka. He is in a striped caftan with a standing collar that he wears over trousers and boots. The most favoured boots were of yellow leather and came from Damascus. He has two gowns over his caftan, one with sleeves. His soft tasselled cap is bound round with cloth.

The woman is a Druse from Damascus. On her head is a *tantour*, a tall silver conical headdress worn by married women. A large gold disk with coins or gold pieces is suspended from it. The headdress would normally have been covered by a large fine white cloth. Headdresses like this were worn by Jewish Algerian women in the nineteenth century. It is sometimes thought that the fifteenth-century tall conical headdress of northern Europe was brought to France by crusaders from the Middle East.

The man on the right is an Arab from Baghdad. He has the many layers so necessary in the desert. A man's weaponry, the way he tied his belt and the way he wore his headcloth would identify where he came from. The caftan is worn with an embroidered jacket over it. The outer gown draped from his shoulders is the *bisht*; another one was often worn under it. On his head is a large cloth held in place by the *agaal*.

THE OTTOMAN EMPIRE

EGYPTIAN BEDOUIN GIRL, FRUIT SELLER AND MESSENGER

• SECOND HALF OF 19TH CENTURY

The Bedouin on the left has the nose-ring traditionally worn by girls, while the belted short tunic is uncommon in female dress, it normally being long and loose. Bedouin dress differed from other dress in this region in being generally baggier, and having longer and more pointed sleeves. The fabrics were usually dark blue or black. A black cotton veil or a mantle was worn over the head. Egyptian Muslim women wore face-veils, complying with certain Koranic laws.

The type worn by the fruit seller probably hangs from a headband, a cord running through a silver tube holding it over the centre of the face. A large mantle covers her house clothes. The messenger on the right is in cotton shirt and baggy trousers; over this he wears an embroidered waistcoat in the Turkish style. The outfit is tied at the waist by a striped sash. His tarboosh has a long silky tassel.

EGYPTIAN MAN AND WOMAN FROM PORT SAID, AND WATER SELLER

• SECOND HALF OF 19TH CENTURY

The woman on the left has a face-veil similar to the woman above. She has tied a simple scarf around her head and wears her sleeveless black mantle open, revealing the *thob*, her top dress. On her arm she carries a large fringed *haik*, or wrap. The man in the middle wears a Western-style shirt. He has a double-breasted waistcoat buttoned up under his jacket. His large finely pleated trousers are very long. Both the jacket and trousers are of white muslin and decorated with braidwork. Around his waist he has a colourful sash, and there are various items tucked into it or suspended from a gold cord around his neck. The blocked red felt hat is a fez.

The water seller wears a long tunic, or *djellaba*, in coarse cotton, over trousers. It has been hitched out of the way into a girdle. He wears a jacket over it. On his head he has wrapped a turban.

EGYPTIAN WOMEN AND MAN

• SECOND HALF OF 19TH CENTURY

The tambourine-playing woman is in a dark robe with wide sleeves, which have been pushed back. On her head is a red and white headcloth; a headpiece of jewellery edged with gold metalwork hangs from this. The triangular pieces hanging in front of the ears are powerful symbols of fertility and ward off the evil eye. The woman in the middle has veiled her face in the same way as in the opposite illustration. She has a white gown over her clothes and a white head-veil.

The servant on the right wears white cotton baggy trousers and a shirt. The waistcoat, which is covered in Turkish-style embroidery, has a row of close-set buttons down the front. The whole is bound around with a striped sash with its tassels hanging down the front. On his shoulders he has a white wrap of wool or cotton, and on his head sits a striped turban.

EGYPTIAN MAN AND WOMEN

• SECOND HALF OF 19TH CENTURY

The Bedouin musician on the left has a long white tunic, which could be of cotton or wool. Over this he has roughly tied a short sleeveless garment. His wrap on top of this is made either from two different materials or else he is wearing two separate garments; the top one is made of a shaggy wool and the bottom one is striped. This layering of the clothing was essential to conserve body moisture, and also as protection against the strong sun and the sand. His headcloth is bound with a red *agaal*.

The woman in the middle is a slave. She is simply dressed in a white robe with a black tunic over it. Her head is covered with a white turban. The woman on the right is in street clothes. Her white *yashmack* is of fine pleated lawn that has been embroidered along the edges. Her cotton robe is also white. Over this she wears a voluminous dark mantle.

Eastern Europe

Eastern Europe has no sea to separate it from Asia. Thus, waves of immigrants were able to come from Asia during the prehistoric period, bringing about the physical and cultural variety of the peoples of Europe.

The region is criss-crossed with river systems, those of the Danube, Vistula, Dnieper and Volga being the principal ones. The Danube runs from western Germany to the Black Sea, passing Vienna, Budapest and Belgrade, and linking eastern Europe with the West. The Vistula played an important part in the history of Poland, the river serving as a trade route from early Stone Age times, with its most intensive development dating from the fifteenth to the eighteenth centuries. Poland was partitioned between Prussia, Austria and Russia at the end of the eighteenth century, and this put an end to the economic importance of the Vistula. Along the Dnieper, a system of river routes developed from the fourth to the sixth centuries, connecting the Black Sea with the Baltic and thus linking the Slavs with both the Mediterranean and the Baltic peoples. Europe's longest river, the Volga, lies further to the east, running north from the Caspian Sea. It was enormously important economically, culturally and historically.

The first Mongol invasions of eastern Europe took place in the thirteenth century. The main aim was to revive the trade that had traditionally crossed the central Asian steppes. Moving ever westwards, the Mongols collaborated with Turkic nomads and Muslim traders along the old Silk Road to achieve this. In the fourteenth century, the Turkic conqueror Timur (Tamerlane; ?1336–1405) took control of the lands of the East after a battle for dominance between the Tartar tribes in the East and in the West, where they controlled the Danube and Dnieper routes and had access to the Crimea.

From the beginning of the Tartar period, there was much disunity among the Russian princes. The princes of Moscow during the first half of the fourteenth century formed an alliance with the great Tartar ruler Öz Beg (ruled 1313–41) and his Crimean supporters. The links forged between Moscow and the Crimea would be important to Moscow's eventual rise as leader of the Russian lands. It meant that furs could be exported through the Crimea to Byzantium, which led to close relations between Moscow and Constantinople.

After the destruction of the Tartar capitals by Timur, it was the combination of an advantageous geographical position, linking Moscow with the major river systems and the steppes, and cunning manoeuvring by the princes, that led to Moscow's dominance. In the fifteenth century, the struggle for this position was won by Ivan the Great (ruled 1462–1505). He turned towards the West. Italian and Greek diplomats and craftsmen were welcomed at court, and he married the Byzantine princess Sofia Palaeologus. Muscovite expansion that had started during his reign was continued under his son Basil III (ruled 1505–33) and his grandson Ivan the Terrible (ruled 1533–84). Ivan the

Russian gentleman, 16th century.

(Background image) Ryazan women, Voronmesh man, Finnish woman and St Petersburg woman, last half of 19th century.

Terrible was the first to use the title of tsar. After he died, a new time of trouble ensued, during which Polish, Swedish and Cossack armies devastated the land.

Poland, Lithuania, Bohemia and Hungary had been loosely associated at the end of the fifteenth century under the rulers of the Polish Jagiellon dynasty, from 1382 to 1572. In 1569, Lithuania and Poland merged their separate institutions by the Union of Lublin. After this, the Orthodox lands of Lithuania would be dominated by Polish nobles and by the Roman Catholic faith. The landowning class, comprising the magnates and the lesser gentry, achieved a political independence that would weaken the power of the monarchy. The towns declined and the peasants were reduced to serfs.

Slavic Bohemia had been allied to both Poland and Germany in its past. In the sixteenth century, the Hapsburgs laid claim to Bohemia and to parts of Hungary, bringing this region firmly into the Western sphere.

In Russia, the Romanov dynasty came to power at the beginning of the seventeenth century after Michael Romanov (ruled 1613–45) succeeded in ejecting the Poles from Moscow. A period of gradual recovery followed; however, apart from a few embassies, Moscow remained fairly isolated from the West.

Eastern European, and especially Russian, dress remained much the same throughout the centuries, with small changes to the details. In the dress of the nobility, use was made of precious materials decorated with metal-thread embroidery, and the application of jewels, spangles and pearls. Seed pearls were reasonably cheap as they came from the rivers flowing into the Arctic Ocean. They were sewn onto all garments but especially headdresses, which were often the most valuable items in the wardrobe. The traditional headdresses showed great regional variation, and were worn on feast days and holidays. During the week, caps and scarves were usually worn. These too varied greatly from region to region, the decoration often revealing the status, religion and origins of the wearer. The peasants produced their garments and furnishings themselves. The most precious garments were often handed down through the generations. These pieces were embroidered and appliquéed with traditional patterns that varied from region to region.

Peter the Great (ruled 1682–89) presided over a period of enormous change. He built up the navy and modernized the army. He reformed the Church and the administration of the government. Cultural life was transformed. He forced his subjects to modernize. Members of the nobility were not only made to shave their beards but also to learn to drink coffee and go to balls in the manner of the West. They had to discard their traditional garments and wear Western-style dress. The urban population soon followed the example of the nobility. By the end of the eighteenth century, even the peasants' traditions and customs had undergone change.

Russian man and women, 17th century (top left); Polish gentleman, 16th century; (top right); Polish man, 17th century (bottom).

EASTERN EUROPE

POLISH GENTLEMAN AND LADY

• SECOND HALF OF 16TH CENTURY

Western European influences, especially from Italy, were strong in aristocratic dress in Poland. The woman has a skirt and laced bodice with the large puffed upper sleeves and fitted lower sleeves of the sixteenth century. Over this is a voluminous sleeveless gown of a patterned fabric, which could be a damask or a brocade. Around her neck is a small ruff of the 1570s, the cuffs following the same shape. Her headdress is a fur-lined cap, which is seen in different versions all over central and eastern Europe.

The man is in a striped caftan, possibly a *doloman*, which is buttoned to the waist to make riding a horse easier. Its stuffed look may indicate that it is lined with heavy wool or fur. Under this his breeches are tucked into boots. He also wears a ruff, and he has a round fur hat. A large fur-lined garment is draped around him.

RUSSIAN AND POLISH GENTLEMEN

• 16TH CENTURY

The Russian is in a striped caftan, possibly a *zipun*, with long sleeves. His cuffs have been turned back, but they were also worn covering the hands. His sleeveless over-gown has a high collar. He has hitched up the front skirts, showing the contrasting lining. Around his waist is a belt, which could be made of leather or be woven, and it is decorated with metal studs of different shapes and sizes. His trousers are hidden under his caftan, but his hose and shoes can be seen. His tall fur-lined cap has a turned-up brim with two points at the front.

The Pole is in a caftan, perhaps a *doloman*, decorated with braided loops and buttons down to the waist. It is made of a rich fabric and is edged with a gold braid; he wears the cuffs turned up. His sword belt is highly decorated: ornate belts were an important part of male dress. Over his caftan, he wears a short-sleeved fur-lined coat with tasselled buttons to the waist. His hose and shoes are similar to the Russian's. His high-brimmed hat has feathers pinned with a brooch at the front.

POLISH MAN AND WOMEN

• 17TH CENTURY

The man wears a caftan, which is perhaps the *zupan*, similar to the Russian *zipun*. This is buttoned from neck to waist beside a decorative braided edge. As was usual, the skirt is unbuttoned, and there is a sash around his waist. Over this he wears a short-sleeved coat, which fastens in the same manner as the garment beneath. The coat has a small standing collar. His breeches are tucked into long tight-fitting boots. Under his wide-brimmed hat he has a skullcap.

The woman's round fur cap and jacket appear to be the only elements of regional dress. She wears her cap over a linen veil, which is draped around her neck like a wimple. The braided fur-trimmed jacket has a lace collar. It was more common to decorate with embroidery in Poland than with lace, which had to be imported. Her bodice with its *pickadils*, or tabbed edge, is shaped like a late sixteenth-century bodice from western Europe. Her lace-trimmed cuffs follow the early seventeenth-century shape. Her skirt looks as if it has a hiproll to support it. The lady in the centre has a large ruff; by 1640, the ruff had all but disappeared in western Europe.

BOHEMIAN WOMAN, GIRL FROM PRAGUE AND SPANISH WOMAN

• FIRST HALF OF 17TH CENTURY

The figures of both the Bohemian woman on the left and the woman from Prague in the middle are based on engravings by Wenceslaus Hollar of 1641 and 1643, representing dress of 1636. In Bohemia, it was especially women of the upper classes who first exchanged their Slavic clothes for German ones. The lower classes retained their traditional dress for much longer. In the sixteenth century, Bohemian dress had already been transformed by outside influences, but not to the extent that it could be confused with German dress.

The Bohemian woman is in a fur-lined mantle that had been worn in the sixteenth century. The fur is seen on the wide revers and flat collar. Under her mantle is a bodice and skirt on more fashionable lines, and a wide piped ruff. Her tall conical fur hat also dates from earlier. The woman from Prague has a flat lace-edged collar over her bodice. Her skirt is covered by a lace-trimmed apron, and her mantle is a shorter version of the mantle on the left.

The Spanish woman wears a striped one-piece gown with a high stiff collar, called a *ropa*, a garment seen in a slightly different form in other western European countries. Her large split sleeves are laced into the gown at the shoulders. The skirt has a train, and at her neck is a small standing lace-edged ruff.

EASTERN EUROPE

TSAR AND BOYARS

• 17TH CENTURY

Russian dress developed from a mixture of native and Byzantine elements. Contemporaries described the richness of the tsar's wardrobe, which was said to be more magnificent than any other ruler's. The dress of the élite consisted of many layers, which, as they restricted movement, indicated status; but they were practical in a cold climate. The tsar wears a rich brocade caftan trimmed with pearls, buttoning down to the hem. Under it he would have at least two shirts, which could be highly ornamented with embroidery and pearls. Caftans of several kinds would be worn over these. On his shoulders rests a collar decorated with icons. His crown is called a *shapka monomakha*. It is made of fur and precious metals, and set with precious stones.

The *boyar* on the left is in a brocade caftan with the characteristic flat sable collar and braided fastenings at the front. The high collar of his undergarment could be detachable. He has a *kolpak*, which is a high fur-edged cap, and boots. The *boyar* on the right is in a different caftan, perhaps a *zipun*; under it is a garment fastened with braided loops and buttons. He has a sash around his waist, red boots and a *kolpak*.

BOYARS AND LADIES

• 17TH CENTURY

The *boyar's* wife in the foreground has a round headdress, which may have originated with the Byzantine diadem, worn over a veil, which would normally have covered her hair. Russian women disguised the shape of their bodies and wore many layers. The figure wears a wide satin caftan, which is buttoned to the ground, with hanging sleeves. Under this, would be several other garments, including chemises and the long sleeveless gown called a *sarafan*. She has a fur-lined muff and a fur-lined brocade mantle.

The *boyar* on the right is in a caftan decorated with flowers. He wears a sword belt with an ornate silver clasp. Over his caftan is a fur-lined mantle with square fur collar and hanging sleeves. He wears a fur-edged cap with a silver ornament.

The man at the centre is much more simply dressed in a woollen gown, which probably opens at the side. He has tucked his dagger into a sash, and he wears a fur-lined coat on top. Like all Russian men, he wears boots.

PRINCE, TORSCHKO LADIES IN SUMMER DRESS AND BELOSERSK WOMAN

• LATE 17TH CENTURY

The prince is wearing a short caftan over wide breeches, which are tucked into high boots. His sleeves almost cover his hands. Over this, he has a black ermine-lined sleeveless coat with loop and button fastenings. A large ermine collar rests on his shoulders and falls down the back. A decorative sword belt is worn around the caftan. His *kolpak* has an ornate silver band.

The women are in summer dress. They have an elaborate pearl-studded high headdress called a *kokoshnik*. An embroidered veil is draped over this. They are dressed in *sarafan* and short caftan. Underneath, the sleeves of the highly decorated outer chemise can be seen; this would have been worn over a plain linen chemise. Over the *sarafan* is a wide sleeveless caftan, which reaches to just below the hips and also buttons down the front. There were many types of caftan, each with slightly different details. Around each of the women's necks is a collar, decorated, like their headdresses, with pearls.

TORSCHKO LADIES IN WINTER DRESS AND RYAZAN WOMAN

• LATE 17TH CENTURY

The little girl wears a calf-length *sarafan* with leggings below. Over this she has a sleeveless caftan showing a plain chemise sleeve. Various unseen layers would have been worn in between the chemise and the outer dress. An edged kerchief covers her head. She has an apron made of a printed fabric. The woman next to her has a long gown and a sleeved short coat with loop fastenings; down her back is a neckerchief in a contrasting colour. Her tall pearl-decorated *kokoshnik* is covered with a heavy veil. She has an embroidered apron. The woman next to them is more richly dressed, in several layers of black fur-trimmed caftans with long sleeves and decorative gold edgings and fastenings. Her *kokoshnik* is shaped differently from her companion's; it is also covered with a thick veil.

The woman on the right is dressed in a sheepskin coat with the wool turned inside. The long sleeves of a colourful chemise are visible at the wrists. Her skirt is woven or printed with a check pattern and edged with different-coloured bands. The apron is decorated with an embroidered and scalloped edge. On her head is a headdress with a multi-coloured fringe at the back; the fringed streamers hanging down her back are embroidered with a cross-hatch pattern.

EASTERN EUROPE

RYAZAN WOMAN, VORONESH MAN, FINNISH WOMAN AND ST PETERSBURG WOMAN

• LAST HALF OF 19TH CENTURY

The linen chemise of the woman from Ryazan on the left is gathered and embroidered with red at the neck and wrists. There is also embroidery on the sleeves. The garment on top with the banded hem is closed at the front; it is probably put on over the head. She has a smock-like apron over this with an embroidered hem. Her outer garment is a coat with short sleeves. On her head is a tall coif with a large shawl draped over it.

The seated woman is from Finland. She has a tall square-crowned headdress wrapped with a linen kerchief. Her patterned skirt can be seen below an over-garment. She wears pearls round her neck. Her coat is edged with a woven braid that ends in tassels.

The woman on the right, from St Petersburg, has a linen chemise gathered at the wrists with embroidered bands and ending in a frill. Over this is a sleeveless bodice and a skirt, edged with a decorative band. Her legs are covered in loose cross-gartered leggings. On her head is a printed kerchief.

MORDVINIAN MAN AND WOMAN, AND ESTONIANS

• SECOND HALF OF 19TH CENTURY

During the long years of Russian domination, Finnish nationalism of any form was strongly discouraged, and the dress of ethnic minorities therefore became greatly simplified. The woman with her back turned is a Mordvinian, of the Volga Finnic peoples. She has an outer coat, which was often made of a felt material, decorated with embroidered and appliquéd borders. Her skirt also has an appliquéd border; below it are leggings cross-gartered with the laces of her soft shoes. Her chemise has an embroidered band round the upper arm. On her head is a cap, called a *pango*. Married women in many cultures had to cover their hair, and in this one it was also necessary to cover the nape of the neck with a decorated flap. A red sash is tied round her waist.

The woman and the seated man together are Estonians, who are also Finnic peoples. The woman's bodice is pinned by a disk brooch. Over her colour-striped skirt is a white apron with an embroidered hem. She has a Russian-looking coat with braided loop fastenings. On her head is a tall headdress not unlike that of the other woman. The man has breeches that are loose at the bottom; hose cover the lower legs. On his feet are soft shoes fastened across the ankles and cloth socks.

JAROSLAV WOMAN, TVER WOMAN, AND KALUGA MAN AND WOMAN

• LAST HALF OF 19TH CENTURY

The women on the left, from Jaroslav and Tver, are wearing *sarafans* over wide-sleeved chemises. The woman on the extreme left has a shorter *sarafan* on top. By the nineteenth century, women's clothes were more revealing, the garments waisted and necks uncovered. Both figures wear a tiara headdress tied at the back with ribbons.

The man from Kaluga is in a Russian shirt that closes at the side. It is tied in at the waist by a sash. His breeches are tucked into his boots. His wife has a tall headdress with a shawl bound over it, the back covering her neck. The sleeves of her chemise are embroidered or sewn with woven bands. Usually, the visible decorated parts of the chemise would be sewn to a plain linen base. The banded hem of her skirt can be seen below a striped apron. Over this is a much richer looking pinafore-type apron. A lined sleeveless coat is worn on top.

CRIMEAN TARTAR WOMAN AND MEN

• LAST HALF OF 19TH CENTURY

The Tartar woman is in a striped skirt over wide pants, called *salwar*, that close at the ankle. She has a wide sleeved chemise that is bound tightly over the forearms. Her bodice is sewn all over with coins. Her headdress consists of a veil draped over a cap that has been sewn with coins; the choker necklace could be a neckpiece attached to the cap. At her waist is a girdle with a round metal clasp.

The man on the right is in a caftan and coat over wide trousers. The caftan has been bound with a wide-striped sash. He has a turban on his head. The man in the middle has wide trousers and a striped garment with a small standing collar that closes on the left side. He wears a fur hat and a striped sash.

Northern Europe

Sweden, Norway and Denmark are closely linked both geographically and historically. Their importance to the rest of Europe lies especially in their geographical position, their lands being situated in both the North Sea and the Baltic Sea.

From very early on, small fishing vessels plied their trade along the coasts of these seas. This was mostly a local activity, but they also went further afield, southwards, and eastwards along the Russian river systems to the Black Sea. Their cargo consisted mainly of fish, meat, fur, wood and salt. Vikings roaming around Europe after AD 800 brought valuable exotic textiles from the south to the north and west. Their own homespun wools and linens were also of a high quality.

During the Stone Age, around 4000 BC, the nomadic culture of the region changed into an agricultural one. By the Bronze Age, between 1800 and 500 BC, a fairly sophisticated culture had developed. After 500 BC, during the Iron Age, the people started to settle in villages.

From the Middle Ages, agriculture was organized collectively. The families of the tenant farmers each used the crops from their own plots, but they worked the fields with others. Resources were shared, and livestock was grazed as a single village herd. It was only in the nineteenth century that this system was dismantled.

In the Middle Ages, it was the Danish kings who dominated north-western Europe. The Frankish expansion brought Denmark into close contact with other European powers, and Christianity reached the region in the ninth century. Sweden was not fully converted until the eleventh century. In the tenth century, King Harald Bluetooth (ruled ?940–?984) unified all of Denmark, and conquered Norway. His son Sweyn (ruled ?985–?1014) and grandson Canute (King of Denmark 1018–35) continually raided England and finally formed an Anglo-Danish kingdom.

During the twelfth century, parts of northern Germany were brought under the Danish crown, and during the thirteenth century Estonia was conquered. Danish domination came to an end in the fourteenth century, when the counts of Holstein ruled the region. It was during this period, and in the following century, that Denmark, Norway and Sweden were united by dynastic ties. This union was broken up by Swedish independence in the sixteenth century, but Norway and Denmark remained together until the early nineteenth century.

Sweden became the dominant power in the Baltic region during the seventeenth century, its influence at one time stretching as far as Poland. Both Sweden and Denmark took on Lutheranism as their state religion at the time of the Reformation.

Norwegian gentleman, first half of 17th century.

(Background image) Northern European men and woman, 3rd–4th century.

NORTHERN EUROPE

Some wool fragments exist from the Neolithic period, but the first well-documented textiles date from the Bronze Age. There are even a few surviving garments from that period. The acid peat bog preserves well such materials as wool and fur. Surviving manufacturing tools include spindles and loom weights. Grave finds indicate that garments were adorned with functional bronze ornaments: pins, brooches and buckles have been discovered, and their location on the bodies has sometimes given a clue as to their use.

Fur, leather, and wool, and later linen, were the materials used for dress during the Bronze Age. The wool was woven in a variety of patterns, and was sometimes dyed. Tablet-woven braids edged some of the garments. Cloaks often fastened with a brooch at the shoulder, and were worn over tunics and leggings or skirts. Cone-shaped caps, hairnets and hoods were used as headgear. Good-quality decorated leather shoes have also been found. As well as the decoration on the shoes and the patterned braids on the clothes, they had wonderful jewellery, which was often set with stones and decorated with spiral patterns.

In later centuries, the close trading links with western Europe meant that, apart from rural dress, fashions followed much the same course in the north as in the rest of Europe. Rural dress showed much regional variation, as was generally the case. The basic elements of men's dress were the coat, jacket and waistcoat, all lavishly decorated with buttons; and trousers, shirt, cap or hat and footwear. It was largely a fossilized form of seventeenth-century dress. By the mid-nineteenth century, rural folk wore almost the same as townspeople. Only the elderly stuck to their traditional headwear: red knitted caps for the men and white linen coifs for the women.

Women's dress consisted of a bodice and skirt, a jacket, apron, shift, coif or scarf and footwear. Until the eighteenth century, only married women covered their hair; young girls wore their hair long, loose or plaited. The women's coif was retained in some areas into the twentieth century. Clogs were usually worn, though on Sundays both women and men wore leather shoes with silver or pewter buckles and clasps. Scandinavian embroidery showed the influence of western Europe, and also followed the fashions of the time.

Man from Jutland, early Bronze Age (top left); Danish woman from Upford, first half of 17th century (top right); Norwegian lady, first half of 17th century (bottom).

NORTHERN EUROPE

TEUTONIC MAN AND WOMAN

• EARLY BRONZE AGE

The clothes of the man and woman in this illustration were based on early Bronze Age discoveries in Jutland and Aarhus. The man was found on Jutland in 1871–5, buried in a tree coffin of the fourteenth century BC. According to the person who found him, he was 'clothed in a tunic which had been held together by a leather belt with a well-preserved wooden button. In the left arm, which was crooked, rested a finely-ornamented wooden scabbard'. His coarse woollen garment was possibly pinned at the shoulders. Around his shoulders was a large semi-circular mantle of coarse wool with the raised pile on the inside. Shoes have been found at other grave sites and there were some leather remains found here. On his head he wore a round woollen cap. He had a bronze sword inside the wooden scabbard.

The woman was found in a grave near Aarhus. She had on a short tunic with short sleeves, with a slit halfway down the front for a neck opening. On her lower half she had a long skirt, gathered around the waist and tied with a long braid girdle ending in tassels. She was found with two hairnets. She had bronze jewellery: an armband, neckband, pin and some disc-shaped ornaments. A small dagger, a horn comb and an urn were also found near her.

TEUTONIC MEN AND WOMAN

• 3RD–4TH CENTURY

Linen perishes in the boggy ground where the bodies of the Scandinavians were found. There survive very few women's garments of this period, and it is therefore thought that many of their garments were made of linen. Some woollen garments have survived, however, and they were usually worn with a girdle and clasped together at the shoulders. Much jewellery has been discovered in burial sites, and brooches have been found at the shoulder position. Buckles have been found near the waist.

The man on the right could have been based on figures on Trajan's Column, where several Germanic men are portrayed. They were auxiliaries in the Roman army, and this might explain the man's tunic, which appears to be covered in metal discs. Several examples of cloth trousers have been found in Denmark with their foot pieces attached to them. Belts have also been found. They were probably of leather and had buckle fastenings. Some were decorated with metal plates.

DANISH MEN AND WOMAN

• 1590

The wide trousers with loose legs appear to have been adopted by seamen in the sixteenth century. There are examples of this seafaring dress quite early in the sixteenth century, but the man on the left has a doublet that identifies him as being from the last quarter. The vertical splits on his doublet are both for decoration and to give ease of movement. The tabbed wings round his shoulders, his tall hat and his small ruff are also of this period.

The woman is in regional dress. Her jacket with its square neck opening is filled in by a decorated separate infill or the edge of her chemise. Her skirt is pleated into the waist and has a fringe around the hem. A fillet holds her hair in place. A large purse and several other items hang from her girdle.

The man on the right is in wide trunkhose, which are in the German style, called *pluderhose*. The lining is cut larger than the panes of the trunkhose, so that it spills out. Below he wears tight-fitting hose and boots, which could be held up by laces tied to the doublet. He wears a doublet with a sleeved jerkin over it.

DANISH WOMEN FROM UPFORD, DITHMARSCHEN AND EIDERSTADT

• FIRST HALF OF 17TH CENTURY

The three women wear headdresses that vary in shape. They are probably all made of starched linen, with the one on the right needing some extra support, either with a stiff material or wiring. Two of the women still have the medieval hooded shoulder capes.

The woman in the middle from Dithmarschen has a jacket that buttons down the front over a tunic that is made of a patterned material. An embroidered pocket hangs from her belt along with a purse and knife. The end of her belt falls alongside the purse strings. Her skirt is evenly pleated all the way around and has a decorative strip down the front. The woman on the left from Upford has a striped bodice and a blue skirt, covered by a white linen apron. The woman on the right has a separate bodice and skirt. Her hooded cape has a fur edge and is perhaps made with chintz material. Chintz was seen increasingly from the seventeenth century onwards, especially in the regions along the northern coast of the Low Countries, and countries like Germany and Denmark that border the North Sea. They all appear to be wearing boots.

NORTHERN EUROPE

NORWEGIAN GENTLEMAN AND LADY WITH CHILD, AND COUNTRY WOMAN

• FIRST HALF OF 17TH CENTURY

The man is wearing a Russian-looking tunic with its braided loop and button fastenings. The tunic is either lined or edged with fur as it has fur cuffs. Over this he wears a fur-lined gown with split sleeves. On his head is a Russian-looking fur-trimmed hat. He has blue hose and leather shoes.

His seated companion has a bodice with a very ornate pattern, which could have been embroidered. She too has fur-edged sleeves. She wears a small piped ruff. Around her shoulders are the false puffs of the chemise. The banded braids along the skirt hem were typical of the end of the previous century. On her head is a padded headdress. The boy has a fur-edged cap with a tassel and a gown with braided decoration following the garment seams. In the background is a country woman with the distinctive cap that was seen in regions all over northern Europe.

DANISH NOBLEMAN AND LADY

• FIRST HALF OF 17TH CENTURY

The man has a well-fitting doublet, with buttons down the front, which ends in a point. The shoulders were widening at this period, and the longer skirts were slit and overlapped. His trunkhose have a thick lining and close above the knees. He wears high boots and inside them boothose, of which the lace-edged cuffs are visible. A cape was still an important feature of male dress. His ruff is small and quite thick. He wears chains and a medallion around his neck, and carries his gloves. His hat has a wide upturned brim and is decorated with feathers.

The woman has a shoulder cape similar to that worn by the woman of Dithmarschen (p. 65), but it is without a hood. She wears it with a skirt that has regular pleats all around and over it an embroidered apron. She has lace-edged cuffs and a thick ruff like her male companion. On her head is a fur-edged cap over a coif. These caps are seen with slight variations all over the colder parts of Europe.

DANISH MAN AND WOMAN, AND WOMAN FROM STAPPENHALL

• FIRST HALF OF 17TH CENTURY

The woman is dressed in a similar fashion to the Danish noblewoman on the previous page, but much plainer. She has the same shoulder cape, which closes in front. Her ruff is the same as well. Her skirt is pleated and worn open at the front, showing an underskirt with its pleats laid flat with bands over them going round the skirt at regular intervals. A third underskirt is showing beneath. On her head she wears a coif with a small hood over it. Around her waist is a metal belt.

The man is in doublet and breeches, known as Venetians which are wide and close below the knee. Whereas the woman has plain linen cuffs, the man's cuffs are edged with what could be Danish bobbin lace. Around his shoulders is a cape that is loosely tied with a cord. His hat is tall with a brim of medium width.

WOMEN FROM SCHLESWIG-HOLSTEIN

• SECOND HALF OF 19TH CENTURY

The woman on the left is in modified fashionable dress of the 1860s. She is missing the wide crinoline and probably wears several layers of petticoats instead. Her jacket is decorated with the silver buttons so beloved by northern Europeans. It has what appear to be the funnel-shaped pagoda sleeves, worn in mainstream fashion during the 1850s and 1860s. The jacket is worn over what could be a bodice decorated with blackwork, with large plain white sleeves. A scarf is knotted in front, and on her head is a small round black cap tied at the side with a black ribbon.

The other woman is in a high-waisted skirt and corset over an underbodice made of a patterned fabric. The skirt is edged with a contrasting colour. She has a colourful scarf around her neck, and many silver charms and medallions hanging about her bodice. On her head is a lace cap. Scarves were sometimes embroidered colourfully on one side and kept in the mourning colours of white, green and blue on the other side. Black leather shoes had silver or pewter clasps for festive dress.

The man is in a short coat with large lapels and silver buttons. He wears a striped waistcoat that closes right up to the neck. He has a black stock over his linen shirt collar. On his head is a knitted cap with a tassel.

German-speaking World

German tribes living along the Rhine were first mentioned by Caesar in about 50 BC. As the Roman Empire came to an end, the Franks, who were settled in Gaul and western Germany, started to expand their kingdom eastwards. In the eighth century, the Carolingian dynasty were the rulers of the Franks. Under Charlemagne (emperor 800–14), their religious, economic and political influence extended from Frisia in the north, Saxony in the east to Bavaria in the south. Each region was left in the hands of counts and bishops, and the local leaders grew more powerful. When the Carolingian line died out, the Saxon dukes took over, the so-called Ottonians. Like Charlemagne, they were awarded by the pope the imperial crown of the Holy Roman Empire.

Germany in the later Middle Ages was chiefly agricultural, but its trade and industry became increasingly important. It benefited from the Hundred Years' War (1337–1453) between France and England, when Mediterranean goods carried northwards passed through their lands instead of up the Rhône valley. Internal warfare between Italian cities also enabled German merchants and financiers to take over as middlemen between Italy and the rest of Europe. North Germany produced mainly staple commodities such as grain, fish, salt and metal.

Apart from the three most important cities of Cologne, Augsburg and Nuremberg, there were many smaller cities. Independent city councils were formed by patrician families, who were later joined by the powerful guilds.

The rule of the Hapsburg Maximilian I (emperor 1493–1519) was dominated by three issues: the reform of the empire's government institutions; the rise of the Hapsburgs to international importance; and the beginnings of the Reformation. Alhough the reforms were not altogether successful, he did increase the dynastic power of his family. Marriage alliances spread Hapsburg influence west and east, and Hapsburg Austria was linked to Spain by the marriage of his son Philip (1478–1506) to Ferdinand and Isabella's daughter Joanna in 1496.

The Reformation was brought about for many different reasons: wide disparities between rich and poor had led to riots and uprisings; the Roman Catholic Church was seen as thoroughly corrupt; and Humanism was changing people's religious needs and expectations. When Martin Luther wrote his 95 theses in 1517, he found fertile ground for his ideas. By the mid-1520s, several German cities and states had cut their ties with Rome and embraced Lutheranism.

At around the same time, the Turks under Suleiman the Magnificent (ruled 1520–66) moved towards the Balkans, Hungary and Vienna. Maximilian's grandson Charles V (1500–58) had to deal with threats from inside and outside his empire. By the end of his

Swiss woman, 17th century.

(background image) Frankish King and Queen, 12th century.

German knight and his daughter, and soldier (top left); German mercenary, first half of 16th century (top right); German woman, 1820s (bottom).

reign, Protestantism had became a fully fledged political movement.

The Thirty Years' War (1618–48) was both a religious war and a struggle for the balance of power in Europe. As in other countries, the importing of precious metals from the New World caused high inflation. Grain prices were especially affected, which meant that less money was available for other products.

At the end of the Thirty Years' War, the empire had fragmented into numerous secular and ecclesiastical principalities and cities. During the seventeenth century, the various states each battled for more power. Prussia's army grew to become the fourth largest in Europe. To pay for it, agriculture and manufacturing were developed. Economic growth was aided by the arrival of large numbers of skilled Huguenot refugees after the revocation of the Edict of Nantes in 1685.

The influence of Louis XIV (reigned 1643–1715) was felt throughout the empire. France became the model for every aspect of life, from elaborate court ceremonial to architecture and dress. Craftsmen specializing in luxury goods found lucrative markets at princely courts. As in France, the cost was borne by the people.

The first half of the eighteenth century saw the various wars of succession as the old imperial lines died out and the balance of power in Europe was again threatened. Prussia and Austria became the dominant powers. The empire had become greatly weakened, and only the protection of Austria kept it safe from its more powerful neighbours. Wars with the new republic of France eventually ended in disaster. The final days of the Holy Roman Empire came in 1805, when Napoleon (1769–1815) descended on Vienna and defeated the combined Russian and Austrian armies.

French occupation provided an example of an efficient centralized government, but the foreign presence aroused a sense of nationality in central Europe. As territorial fragmentation ceased, the idea of political unity became a real possibility.

After the defeat of Napoleon, the Congress of Vienna (1814–15) redrew the map of Europe. Germany now had 39 states, ranging in size from Austria and Prussia to small principalities and cities. Austria surrendered its possessions in southern and western Germany and the Austrian Netherlands for Venetian territory on the Adriatic, and its interest shifted eastwards. With territories along both the eastern and western borders, the kingdom of Prussia occupied the pivotal postition in the nation.

Large-scale industry was introduced in central Europe, and railroads, highways and canals were constructed. A new and influential middle class was born; but the new stability remained shaky, with a large peasant population that had too little land, and a body of skilled artisans who could not compete with the factories.

GERMAN-SPEAKING WORLD

FRANKISH KING AND QUEEN

• 12TH CENTURY

The figure of the queen is based on a sculpture from Notre Dame de Corbeil in the Louvre, Paris. The shape of dress was fairly constant up to this period. Tunics had long sleeves; women wore them long, men either short or long. The mantle was usually pinned at the right shoulder. The overall silhouette remained the same, though during the eleventh century a slight slimming down in the volume of the fabric occurred, and there were the beginnings of hanging sleeves and tighter waists. In the first half of the twelfth century, men started to wear longer tunics, and there was a perceptible tightening up of the silhouette.

The change was more marked for women, though it only affected the upper classes. Clothes were worn much tighter and accentuated the body shape. The bodice had a honeycomb texture, perhaps owing to smocking that gave elasticity to the material. The robe had long close-fitting sleeves, widening out at the bottom. Sometimes they were so long and wide that the sleeves were knotted to prevent them from trailing along the ground. The skirt was cut wide and fell in folds to the ground. Women were hardly ever without a head-covering, which was sometimes secured by a fillet. Cloaks varied in length; they were always rectangular, and were fixed with pins or brooches.

JEW, COMMONER AND KNIGHT

• 12TH CENTURY

In medieval images, Jews can be recognized by the pointed hat, the *Judenhut*. Its shape varied from a simple cone to the more complicated pointed models. The earliest illustrations of Jewish hats are seen in the eleventh century. In some regions, Jews were obliged to display a badge, which usually took the form of a white circle.

The figure in the middle is wearing a Jewish hat; the rest of his clothing appears to be ordinary dress. The textile of his tunic is patterned, with a decorative band around the sleeve. The commoner on the left wears a plainer garment, which he has hitched up to show the way in which his hose have been attached to the girdle; the girdle also holds his loincloth in at the waist. The man on the right is dressed more luxuriously in a patterned tunic, which is split for riding. The slashed-hem decoration is called dagging and was more common in the fourteenth and fifteenth centuries. His cloak is probably lined with fur.

GERMAN PRINCE AND LADIES

• 13TH CENTURY

The silhouette now had narrow shoulders and had widened at the hem. Clothes were more tailored, the skirt widened by the use of gores. Both wool and silk might be patterned, but silk patterns were generally more complicated. On top of the gown, a new type of garment was worn: the surcoat. Of an A-shape, it was worn by both sexes. It could be cut out at the sides or have false sleeves that were let hang. Long cloaks over this were cut on a semi-circle rather than the twelfth-century rectangle. They were secured by a cord at the front.

With statues of this period, most figures held the cord of the cloak away from the throat with their thumb in a characteristic gesture. The female headdress consisted of a band of linen, or *barbette*, under the chin, a veil or hairnet and a decorative fillet to hold it all together. The hair was either pinned on the top of head or covered with a net, or it hung loose down the back. Men were usually depicted bare headed, but there were felt hats, which at that time were generally covered with silk or, according to one account, with peacock feathers.

GERMAN KNIGHT AND HIS FAMILY

• 13TH CENTURY

The principal difference now between male and female clothing was in the length. Women, who did not have to do manual labour, wore trailing robes; men never wore their gowns below ankle length.

The man on the left is wearing a sleeveless surcoat over his hauberk. It is from this kind of garment, which appeared in the early thirteenth century, that the word coat of arms stems. It would be of silk or linen. Heraldry originated during the twelfth century, one reason for this being the popularity of the tournament. The helm (closed helmet), placed on the column, was worn by knights; it too was decorated to identify the wearer. The man on the right is wearing a *chapel*, a type of helmet that remained in use until the sixteenth century. He wears this over a full suit of mail: the hauberk, coif and *chausses*, which are hose of mail. Children wore a smaller version of adult clothes.

GERMAN-SPEAKING WORLD

GERMAN KNIGHT, GÜNTHER OF SCHWARZENBURG, MAN AND WOMAN

• SECOND HALF OF 14TH CENTURY

The illustration of Günther of Schwarzenburg on the right is based on his grave monument in the Cathedral of St Bartholomew, Frankfurt, 1352. From the 1340s, great changes in costume took place as tailoring became more in evidence. The padded doublet, or *jaque*, which was originally worn under the armour, now developed as outer wear. It was cut close to the body and had long tight sleeves, becoming shorter and more waisted during the century. Contemporary commentators deplored the new fashions: the doublets worn by young men were so narrow and short that they could not be put on without help; their belts were as wide as horse leathers and had huge buckles. The belts were worn ever lower on the hips, giving a much longer look to the torso.

Female dress moved in the same direction as male dress. The lady in the illustration is wearing an outer robe, called a cotehardie. It has wide sleeves, showing the long tight sleeves of her under robe, the kirtle. The sleeves cover the knuckles. At this period, the outer robe often had short sleeves with strips of fabric, known as tippets, hanging from them, For the first time, women's dress had a wide deep neckline. Buttons were now an important feature of both male and female dress. They were both decorative and functional, and they helped to make these tight clothes easier to wear.

GERMAN NOBLEMAN AND CITIZEN

• SECOND HALF OF 14TH CENTURY

The new fashions in dress remained the preserve of the élite, and long gowns were still worn by officials and older men. The gowns the men wear in this illustration are baggier than was then fashionable, and they were perhaps being worn over a padded doublet. Their heavy belts are worn low on the hips, one of the men having a large pouch attached to his. An Italian writer was particularly critical of these 'enormous German bags'.

Cloaks were cut in a circle and fastened at the front or buttoned on the right shoulder, as here. A shoulder cape, called a gorget, with a hood attached, had been worn for several centuries, but the hood now developed a long tail, called a liripipe.

Hose were cut on the cross to give greater elasticity and were now attached by lacing to the doublet. This produced a tighter, less wrinkled appearance. The men both have small round berets with upturned brims.

GERMAN LADY AND GENTLEMAN

• MIDDLE OF 15TH CENTURY

By the fifteenth century, clothes had lost their exaggerated elongation. The wider over-gown, the *houppelande*, was part of the new look. It first appeared at the end of the fourteenth century, and was worn by both men and women. It had long hanging sleeves that could trail along the ground. It usually had a high collar, which was sometimes turned down. At the beginning of the century, men wore it both long and short with a girdle on the hips. By the 1430s, it had lost its train and was often worn knee length with a long girdle. Women wore their girdle very high under the breast, giving them a pregnant appearance. They had the fourteenth-century kirtle on under their *houppelande*.

Decoration at this period was created by dagging, cutting and slashing the borders of the garments. The man at the centre has a baldrick slung diagonally across his chest, to support the sword, dagger or pouch. At this period, both baldricks and belts were often decorated with bells.

Many different-shaped hats and headdresses were worn, including broad-brimmed straw hats like the one worn on the left. The same man has the typical mid-century sack-like sleeves to his costume, tight at the wrist and widening out over the elbow.

GERMAN JUDGE, CITIZEN AND PEASANT

• SECOND HALF OF 15TH CENTURY

The peasant's dress of doublet, hose and hood had not changed much since the previous century. Working people always did wear their clothes shorter, for convenience sake. The components of the peasant's dress on the right are not very different from those of his wealthier contemporaries, but they are of a poorer cloth. He still wears the gorget and hood around his shoulders, whereas the headwear of the upper classes had changed. His doublet is padded and he has a belt with a leather pouch and a dagger. He protects his lower legs in the old way with cloth and binding.

The man in the middle probably has a woollen fur-lined gown on over his doublet and hose; the judge has a hooded gown with hanging sleeves over his. On his head the judge wears a tall brimless hat, probably made of felt, with a ridge on the crown. On the floor are wooden pattens, worn over the indoor shoes to protect them from the outside dirt. Pointed shoes had now become fashionable.

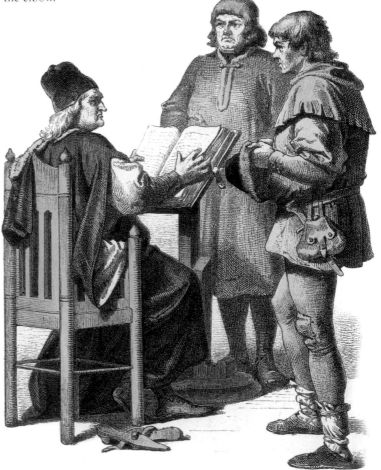

GERMAN-SPEAKING WORLD

GERMAN PATRICIAN MAN AND WOMAN

• END OF 15TH CENTURY

The woman is wearing a padded headdress consisting of about seven layers of linen, visible at the front; around this and her chin is bound a linen cloth. She wears a kirtle of patterned silk, and a gown over this with a high waistline and a V-shaped neck. The headdresses of German women varied according to the region they came from. This padded headdress was worn in the south.

Men now wore low-cut waist-length doublets with large sleeves. As the doublet was a close-fitting garment, it was often split in various places for ease of movement. This became a decorative feature, displaying the fine linen beneath. The hose are visible in their full length, and the two legs were no longer separate, although in Germany they were now often split into upper and nether hose. A flap at the front grew into a pouch known as the codpiece. In the illustration, a cloak is slung over the man's right shoulder.

GERMAN PATRICIAN MAN AND WOMAN

• END OF 15TH CENTURY

The old man is wearing a chaperon over a coif, a development of the shoulder cape and hood that was put on first. With the help of a padded roll, it assumed a large turban-like shape; the liripipe was draped around the shoulders, and the shoulder cape stuck out of the top. It was a type of headdress that stayed in use much longer in southern Germany than elsewhere. Older men retained the long gown, worn here with a sleeveless overgarment called a *huke*.

The woman is wearing one of the last types of fifteenth-century stiff headdress. It was created by folding starched cloths over a headdress, not by wiring. Different variations of this style existed. Nuremberg women wore these to church.

It had for long been normal practice to attach various articles to the belt, the most common items being the dagger and the purse. Purses were made of all kinds of material, including velvet, cloth and leather, and were decorated in different ways. They varied from a leather bag with a flap to a drawstring pouch.

GERMAN PRINCELY COUPLE

• FIRST HALF OF 16TH CENTURY

Until the 1530s, young women preferred low necklines. Thereafter, like the older women, they filled in the neck opening with the edge of the chemise, or with a separate infill. The infill could be square or V-shaped. It was made of a stiff underlayer covered with silk. It was usually a different colour from the bodice, and was sometimes embroidered, or stitched with pearls and precious stones. The gown itself had a large heavy skirt. Braid trimming was used along the hem, neck and sleeves. Women wore the flat men's beret during the first half of the sixteenth century.

German armour is recognizable by its use of ribbed surfaces. The prince in the illustration wears what is known as Maximilian armour. This style remained fashionable from the end of the fifteenth century to the middle of the sixteenth century. Its bulbous breastplate, large skirt pieces and upstanding shoulder pieces are characteristic of this type of armour. Armour always followed the shape of the fashionable silhouette in its broad outline, and the foot pieces with their wide blunt toes were the same shape as shoes at this period.

GERMAN PEASANT COUPLE

• 16TH CENTURY

Peasant dress differed from that of the upper classes in its old-fashioned and plainer style, and its coarse homespun materials. The woman's kirtle is sleeveless and shows the sleeves of her chemise, which would be of coarse linen. The bodice would be front fastening for convenience. The skirt is ankle length; older women would wear it to the feet. Often they would tuck their skirt into the waistband to reveal the underskirt. Her apron is pleated into a small yoke and hangs from her neck. It would be made of linen or canvas. A neckerchief is worn over the shoulders; the headdress could be a simple veil or a kerchief.

Men still wore a short garment like the medieval tunic, either with or without a belt. The man is wearing a garment that could be the doublet itself or an overgarment. It would be made of a coarse woollen fabric or leather. Legs were covered in long hose, sometimes with soles attached and worn without shoes. Boots of all kinds might be worn. The type worn by the man illustrated were often attached to the waist girdle. A hooded cape was still worn for extra protection.

GERMAN-SPEAKING WORLD

GERMAN MERCENARIES

• FIRST HALF OF 16TH CENTURY

Although the mercenary, or *landsknecht*, is commonly credited with spreading the idea of slashed garments, this fashion had already started to appear in civilian dress at the end of the fifteenth century. However, it is true that the characteristic image of the sixteenth-century *landsknecht* is the soldier in very elaborately slashed dress. In contrast to the bourgeois and the nobleman, the soldier usually wore just doublet and hose. The soldiers in this illustration wear pieces of mail and plate armour over their doublets. There was enormous variety in the slashing of *landsknecht* clothing. Short or long, on a slant or straight, close together or far apart, the splits in the fabric created marvellous patterns. Hose were often striped on one leg. There was no uniformity in their dress, for the *landsknechte* were allowed to do as they wished. The regimental system was still unknown, and there was little discipline.

Bourgeois and noble dress became increasingly plain towards the middle of the century, through the influence of Protestantism and sober Spanish dress. With the dress of *landsknechte*, however, decorative slashing was in use for a long time. It continues up into the berets of these soldiers. Feathers hanging over the edge of the brim balance the wide berets.

GERMAN MEN AND WOMEN

• FIRST HALF OF 16TH CENTURY

The jerkin was a close-fitting garment that often had a pleated skirt and was worn over the doublet. It was usually cut low and wide at the front, and could be with or without sleeves. A short gown was worn over these two garments. From the beginning of the sixteenth century, sleeves became large and puffed. Civilian hats and bonnets had slashed brims like the soldier's beret; both men and women might wear them over a hairnet of gold, silver or silk cords that was laid over a coloured-silk base. The bonnet, the wide shoulders, the hem of the jerkin and gown, and the blunt shoes accentuated the horizontal line that was characteristic of the first half of the sixteenth century.

Accessories such as the large ornate purses, the many heavy chains and the elaborate slashing distinguished the Germans from other Europeans. Women's gowns were still high-waisted, with the emphasis on the stomach produced by the heavy skirts. The woman on the left has a feathered hat rather like the soldier's beret. The woman on the right wears a padded headdress seen only in Germany.

GERMAN CAVALRYMEN AND LADY

• SECOND HALF OF 16TH CENTURY

The dark colours and strong tight lines of Spanish dress were a strong influence on the rest of Europe, but shapes were also influenced by other fashions. Around 1570, the frilled edge of the chemise changed into a starched ruff. It was worn above the high collar of the doublet. The linen of the chemise, which burst out of the shoulder joins between the sleeves and the bodice, now developed into padded rolls, or wings.

The short puffed trunkhose were cut in panes or strips, revealing the lining. In German fashion, a contrasting lining was cut larger than the panes and spilled out through them. These trunkhose were called *pluderhosen*. The fashion for them is said to have been spread by the *landsknechte*. The codpiece was still in evidence. Hose were now knitted more often than not, as they gave the clean tight line that was preferred at this period. Boots were of good-quality leather and fitted the legs closely; they could be attached to the trunkhose by laces. From the 1560s and 1570s, the flat berets were often replaced by high toques, which were covered in fabric. The berets that survive have a slightly puffed look. Feathers were placed at the side, and the hats worn at a jaunty angle.

GERMAN NOBLEMAN AND LADY FROM THE PALATINATE

• SECOND HALF OF 16TH CENTURY

The lower part of the doublet started to be padded at this period, and would eventually give the doublet its curious peascod shape at the end of the century. Sleeves were sometimes laced onto the doublet, but were now more often attached to the body of the jacket. Jerkins or gowns could be worn over the doublet, or, as here, a short fur-lined cloak, which might have sleeves. These short cloaks were a Spanish fashion seen everywhere in Europe. Shoes were decorated with small splits, and could be covered in silk or be made of leather.

Women's bodices were similar to the man's doublet and ended in a point at the front. They were stiffened with steel or whalebones. Under the skirt was a cone-shaped hooped petticoat called a farthingale. The lady in the illustration wears a short jacket cut wide at the back, with large puffed sleeves cut high on the arm to show the doublet sleeves below. Her head is covered in a jewelled hairnet, which she wears in combination with a small beret borrowed from male dress.

GERMAN-SPEAKING WORLD

GERMAN MEN AND WOMAN

• FIRST HALF OF 17TH CENTURY

Instead of the slashing and paning of the sixteenth century, clothes were now trimmed with braid and lace. French fashions would dominate as the century progressed. Men's dress during the first half of the century still consisted of the doublet and hose. Breeches started to appear, and cloaks were much worn. All had matching trimmings. The doublet with its skirt of short, squared tabs was worn over the shirt. The sleeves of the doublet were plain and fitted, and buttons were generally used as fastenings.

The man on the right has a semi-circular collar, made of linen or lawn and trimmed with lace, that is probably resting on a wire frame. The cloak has decorative fastenings thought to be influenced by eastern European dress. It reaches to the knees and has a flat 'sailor collar'. The wide breeches match his doublet. Garters tied in large bows below his knees hold up the hose. The seated man has a thick ruff around his neck and is wearing a cloak. Both men have large wide-brimmed hats with high crowns.

The woman has a matching bodice and skirt, the skirt hitched up to reveal her petticoat. Her low, square neck has been filled in with a neckerchief, and she has a similar collar to her companion. Her headdress is probably particular to her region.

WOMEN FROM MUNICH, NUREMBERG AND VIENNA

• FIRST HALF OF 17TH CENTURY

The illustrations are based on engravings by Wenceslaus Hollar of 1643 and 1649, representing Bohemian dress of 1636.

In rural areas, women's regional dress was less like contemporary fashion than in towns. The various towns showed slight differences from each other in the accessories. The fashion for the large ruffs and collars of the three ladies illustrated was coming to an end by this time. The hats may be the regional element in their dress. Fur hats of different shapes are seen in sixteenth-century illustrations of women from Franconia to Livonia. The rest of their dress conforms with bourgeois dress elsewhere. They wear front-laced bodices with separate skirts. Short cloaks with flat collars were lined with fur or a rich silk, as worn by the woman on the left. Her skirt and cloak are decorated with braiding, and her apron is edged with lace. All three might be wearing padded rolls around their hips to give their skirts the desired shape.

SWISS BRIDE, MAN AND WOMAN

• 17TH CENTURY

The bride wears a gown over her bodice and skirt, which are evidently of a precious material. The gown has sleeves that were at the height of fashion in the 1580s; her thick ruff and lace-trimmed cuffs were more common in the 1630s. Wedding crowns of different sorts, with or without veils, were seen all over northern Europe. They were often decorated with flowers and tinsel, and could be of metal or made from a stiffened cylinder covered with fabric. Both brides and grooms wore them. A bride traditionally gave a wreath of natural or artificial flowers and a decorative handkerchief to the groom.

The man on the left of the bride is dressed in the doublet, breeches and cloak of the 1630s and 1640s. His ruff, too, is of the 1630s. The woman on the right has a garment of a more curious shape. Her sleeve has the split down its length that is seen elsewhere, but her long pointed bodice, which is cut high up by a girdle, is unusual, and is perhaps an element of regional dress.

STRASBOURG CONSUL AND COUNCILLOR

• SECOND HALF OF 17TH CENTURY

During the 1660s, men started to wear different clothes. A longer looser coat replaced the doublet, which up until then had been seen in various different shapes. The coat hung to just below the knees. Generally without a collar, it had buttons down the front from neck to hem. The pockets were set low, with the openings buttoned rather than with flaps. The coat had elbow-length sleeves with deep turned-back cuffs. Under the coat was a sleeved waistcoat, cut along the same lines as the coat and the same length.

Around their necks the men wore bib-shaped, falling bands, meeting edge to edge in front. Tasselled strings tied the collar under the chin. The sleeves often had frills, but sometimes they were worn without, ending instead in a small cuff. On their heads they had very broad-brimmed hats with a shallow round crown. The long, shoulder-length, curly hair of both men in the illustration are probably wigs.

GERMAN-SPEAKING WORLD

GERMAN SOLDIERS FROM WÜRTTEMBERG

• FIRST HALF OF 18TH CENTURY

Until the beginning of the eighteenth century, military dress was not very different from civilian dress. It was Frederick William I (King of Prussia 1713–40), influenced by the Swedish army, who transformed the Prussian army, which in its turn would influence other armies. He took great pains creating a uniform. By 1729, the Prussian army's coats were said to be cut so short, and so small in body and sleeves, that the soldiers had trouble putting them on. Their hats were three-cornered, officers, with gold or silver lace around the brim, the men, with yellow or white tape. Their hair was tied back into a tail and powdered. One or two small curls were worn at each side. The waistcoats, breeches and gaiters were generally white. It was an important part of army discipline to keep them white.

In Württemberg, in 1724, the uniform had not yet reached the extremes of the Prussian army. The coats had ample skirts that could by buttoned back for convenience. The officer's hair in the illustration has been tightly bound with ribbon. Military dress, like working men's and sportmen's dress, was to have an enormous influence on male dress during the second half of the eighteenth century.

GERMAN WOMEN FROM LUDWIGSBURG, MUNICH AND THE BLACK FOREST

• SECOND HALF OF 18TH CENTURY

Although the two town girls on the left do not have the extreme hairstyles of the time, they are dressed according to the fashion of the 1780s. The girl in the middle is wearing a jacket and petticoat over a bodice that dips to a point. The bodice is laced over a stiff piece at the front called a stomacher. Her low neckline is covered by a kerchief that is pinned together. The girl on the left has a pretty petticoat, with a floral pattern embroidered or woven into it. Her jacket has a small peplum at the back. Her kerchief crosses the front and is tied behind. The kerchiefs and the ruffles falling from the women's sleeves are probably of a washable material such as lawn or cambric. The fabrics of their jackets are striped, a style that was seen increasingly during the 1780s. Their caps are probably cotton too. Aprons were an important accessory during the eighteenth century, both for practical and for decorative purposes.

The peasant girl on the right is in the regional dress of the Black Forest. She wears a waistcoat over a bodice, and a skirt that is hitched up and held by a decorative belt. Her plait is threaded with a long ribbon, and she has a straw hat.

AUSTRIAN INFANTRYMAN AND HUSSAR

• 1760–75

The Austrian uniform coat was usually white, with the coloured facings, collar and cuffs of the regiment. The Hungarian regiments were an exception until the mid-eighteenth century, when their coats conformed to the standard white. The Staff Infantry had a blue coat and waistcoat with red collar and cuffs. It is not clear what regiment the soldier on the right belonged to. His cap with the false front made of leather has a brass plate bearing the imperial cypher of the double-headed eagle.

Hussars originally came from Hungary and were the light cavalry regiments of the Austrian army. During the eighteenth century, there were hussars in the French, Russian and Prussian armies. The uniform developed from their national dress: the short braided jackets with fur-edged braided pelisses on top, which were either slung over a shoulder or worn, as here, like a jacket. The Hungarian shaggy cap was replaced by a peakless felt shako with a black and yellow rosette and cords. Their plaits were said to protect against sabre cuts. The bag the hussar carried on his back was his sabretache. Originally a sack carried on the sword belt, it became a decorative piece, and was embroidered with emblems and cyphers. The hussar, on the left, is from the 34th Regiment, which had a parrot-green uniform with red breeches and light blue shako.

GERMAN GIRL AND WOMAN, AND ARMY POSTMASTER AND POSTILLION

• END OF 18TH CENTURY

The girl on the left is in an open robe and petticoat. The sprig-printed fabric would probably be a cotton. Her fichu is tied in front. The high puff bonnet is decorated with ribbons and flowers. Her companion is in a fashionably striped closed gown. Her fichu is edged with a Classical braid, and has a heavy border and a fringe at the ends. At her neck is a lace jabot. She has a fob hanging from her belt. Her tall hat was borrowed from men's dress, and it has a cockade.

The men are in uniform. They are both involved in the postal sevice; the man on the left is an army postmaster and the man on the right is a postillion. Their hats were also worn by civilians. The bicorne hat was especially fashionable in the 1780s, and was worn both across the head and with the points front and back.

GERMAN-SPEAKING WORLD

SWISS COUPLE FROM SCHAFFHAUSEN AND WOMAN FROM APPENZELL

• END OF 18TH CENTURY

The Schaffhausen couple on the left are taken from a portrait by Joseph Reinhardt (1713–93) in Berne. Folk dress all over Europe developed with the growing prosperity of the peasants. Before the eighteenth century, rural clothes were virtually the same as those worn in towns, but cruder in cut and of coarser materials; from that period, the style of rural dress started to fossilize. Class, marital status and religion were indicated in various details.

On ordinary working days, clothes of homespun cloth were worn. For Sundays, high festivals, christenings, weddings and burials, great care was taken with dress, which would often be made of fine cloth. Dress in winter differed little from summer, with layers being added or removed. The basic components of female dress were the corset, jacket, skirt, apron and coif.

The couple from Schaffhausen are dressed for church. She wears a big fur bonnet called a *Hinderfür* (meaning 'back to front'); this was worn in summer as well. Men of Schaffhausen wore wide linen breeches, usually black, with white stockings. A scarlet woollen waistcoat was worn over the shirt.

SWISS COUPLE FROM UNTERWALDEN AND WOMAN FROM FRIBOURG

• END OF 18TH CENTURY

The man from Unterwalden on the left is wearing dress of the late eighteenth century: coat, breeches and waistcoat. Over these he has a cloak with tasselled fastenings, called *Brandenburgs*. The women wear several petticoats. On ordinary days, the uppermost one would be working dress. Earlier, aprons were of homespun linen; later, they were made of printed calico, fine wool or silk.

The Fribourg woman on the right is in Sunday dress. She wears a red corset that laces at the front, a black jacket and a red striped skirt. Her apron is black. Her small ruff seems to be a detail left over from sixteenth-century dress. Her cylindrical headdress indicates that she is a German speaker; the French-speaking women of Fribourg wore large flat hats, trimmed with lace.

The Unterwalden woman has an eighteenth-century tricorne hat; her bodice is laced in front. She wears a striped skirt and apron. The stripes often indicated the region from which the wearer came: broad stripes in some places, narrow in others.

GERMAN GENTLEMAN AND LADIES

• BEGINNING OF 19TH CENTURY

The man in a dark-coloured frock coat, pantaloons and hessian boots acts as the perfect foil to the ladies, who, in softly draped white muslin, are dressed in imitation of antique marble statuary. Ladies at this period had a high-waisted narrow silhouette. Their hair was cut very short and curled, or it was left long and bound in the antique manner. Most wore a chemise, petticoat and stays beneath their muslin gowns, though some discarded them. Low necklines were often filled in during the day with a tucker, as worn by the seated figure.

The lady with the parasol is probably wearing a pelisse, a coat-like garment that follows the shape of her dress. Her skirt trails along the ground, as was the fashion until about 1808, when skirts were shortened to above the feet. Her straw bonnet is decorated with flowers. The lady on the right is in evening dress. On her head is a turban, over which she has draped a veil. The favourite and fashionable item for warmth was the Indian shawl. The best-quality ones came from Kashmir, but both England and France were producing their own versions of them by the end of the eighteenth century.

GERMAN LADIES

• 1810s

During the 1810s, Romantic influences began to appear in styles of dress. Decorations harked back to the sixteenth and seventeenth centuries. The three ladies are dressed for outdoors. The lady on the left is in a pelisse dress; the other two are wearing spencers, which are short jackets, following the lines of the bodice, with long sleeves. The waistline was still high, but the skirt was now short enough to reveal the feet. Shoes were flat.

The woman's silhouette was changing at this date from long and draped to a more solid cone shape. Instead of floaty muslins, women wore stiffer cottons and silks. Gothic Vandyke edging, lace trimming, ruching and ruffs were in evidence. They were layered around the neck, sleeves and hem. The tall-crowned bonnets had wide brims that enclosed the face. The ribbon bows, the feathers and flowers that trimmed the hats heightened them even further.

GERMAN-SPEAKING WORLD

BAVARIAN CAVALRYMEN

• FIRST QUARTER OF 19TH CENTURY

The soldier in the middle, in a green jacket with red facings and white buttons, is from the National Chevau-Légers. Their shako had a plume, white loop and button over a crowned brass plate with the letters MJK, as on the sabretache of the man on the right. This soldier is a hussar, and his black shako could indicate that he is of the 1st Regiment. His dolman and pelisse are blue with white buttons and lace, and edged with black fur. His shako has a white and blue plume and white cords.

The soldier on the left is an Uhlan. Originally the Uhlans were a Polish light cavalry regiment in the service of Saxony. By the middle of the eighteenth century, the Austrian and French armies had Uhlan regiments too. Their costume consisted of a fur-trimmed cap with a square crown known as a *czapka*. The Bavarian uniform was copied from the Austrian Uhlans'. The soldiers wore a yellow-topped *czapka* with white piping and cords, and blue and white plume. Their coats and breeches were dark green with light blue collar, cuffs, facings and stripes. Their buttons were white, and the waist sash was white and light blue. Details of these uniforms, such as the shape of the shako and the pelisse, would have an influence on mainstream fashion.

GERMAN GENTLEMAN AND LADIES

• 1820s

The man has the typical silhouette of the 1820s: sloping shoulders, rounded torso and small waist. His coat has a high shawl collar, enhancing the effect of the low shoulders, which are widened with padding. Ankle- and knee-length pantaloons were being gradually replaced by trousers. The trousers of the 1820s were full at the waist and narrowed towards the feet, where they were strapped under the boot. The collar of the shirt was still attached, and worn with a fine white linen cravat. The top hat was worn throughout the century, but gradually changed its proportions.

In 1820, women's waistlines began to drop. The longer bodices would now be fastened at the back with hooks and eyes. During the day, the bodices were worn closed at the throat. The shoulder line was widened by adding extra fullness to the sleeves. Skirts were gored, and flared out towards the hem. All this widening required extra support, which was achieved with starching, quilting and padding.

The ladies in the illustration have puffed shoulders and padded decoration along the hem. The black silk spencer of the figure in the middle has V-shaped decoration, which widens her bodice still further. The taste for the Gothic continued: the lady on the right has a so-called Mary Stuart cap under her large-feathered hat. Heavily trimmed hats echoed the widened shoulders and hems.

BAVARIAN WOMEN

• SECOND HALF OF 19TH CENTURY

Women's clothes were made either of wool, a mixture of wool and linen, cotton or silk. All colours were used, but the most common ones were black, white, green and blue.

The women here have skirts and bodices with a corset on top. The corsets have shoulder straps, and are fastened with lacing or with hooks and eyes, in front or down the side. They could be covered with wool or velvet, and plain as here or decorated. They have square neckerchiefs that have been folded in half and crossed in front, with the ends tucked into the corset. Stockings were usually plain, but in some parts of Bavaria blue and white ones, as here, were worn. Felt hats were worn all over Germany; in the south they were like men's hats, whereas in the north they were more like bonnets. The ones in the illustration are covered with green cloth and decorated with ribbons of the same material. Working dress was plainer than festive dress, and these women would probably have worn more decorative corsets, aprons and neckerchiefs on Sundays.

BAVARIAN MEN

• SECOND HALF OF 19TH CENTURY

In the mountain areas of Bavaria, Switzerland and Austria, breeches were not gathered into a band but open at the bottom, showing the knees. They were made of velvet, plush, wool or leather, with the seams picked out in white stitching. The bib and the pockets were often embroidered with floral patterns. Different regions used different colours and materials. Stockings, decorated with a green or blue loop-pattern, covered the lower legs, leaving the knees and sometimes the ankles bare. Mountain shoes were heavy and hobnailed. On Sundays, men wore waistcoats, but on working days they would usually wear just jackets.

The man on the left has on an open waistcoat under his jacket. In Bavaria and Tyrol, these are known as *Joppen*, and are made of thick wool, or *Loden*. The Bavarian *Joppen* are the longest, and have a standing collar and lapels, and horn buttons. Over this, shepherds and hunters wore a poncho-like cloak of *Loden*. The round felt hat was decorated with a feather and usually with a cord as a hatband.

GERMAN-SPEAKING WORLD

SWISS WOMEN FROM ST GALLEN AND SCHAFFHAUSEN

• SECOND HALF OF 19TH CENTURY

The girl from St Gallen, who has her back turned, is wearing a jacket with three-quarter-length sleeves. The sleeves of her chemise show below. She has a corset with shoulder straps over this, which is covered with a decorative material, either printed or woven. Around her shoulders is a plain fringed kerchief. Her skirt and apron are also plain. Her decorated corset, pearl necklace and earrings suggest that she is dressed in her Sunday best. On her head is a cap of black tulle, topped by a very small white mobcap trimmed with long black ribbon streamers.

Her companion from Schaffhausen has the usual skirt, apron and blouse. Over her blouse, which closes high on the neck, is a black frilled bodice. It is held in place by the corset, which is laced with red laces. The corset is decorated with silver medallions, amulets and chains. She is carrying a wide straw hat.

AUSTRIAN MAN AND WOMAN FROM TYROL

• SECOND HALF OF 19TH CENTURY

The man from the Grödner valley in Tyrol is dressed in a frock coat. Underneath, he has a shirt with a large turned-down collar, a waistcoat and black breeches. Around his neck is a black cravat. On his head is a tall wide top hat, with a wide hatband held by a large silver buckle. He has white stockings and black pumps. Belts were an important part of German regional dress only in Tyrol, where they were prized items. They were richly decorated, every belt being slightly different, and usually of leather. Here it is wide and straight, with a silver buckle and tip.

The woman has a long jacket with green and red cuffs over a multi-coloured bodice. The laced-up corset opening is wide. Her black skirt is covered almost completely by a damask apron. Her silver girdle has several ornate pendant pieces. She wears a very wide, green hat. The ruff was usually only seen in the north of Germany, but the Grödner valley was an exception. It falls in fan-shaped pleats from a flat standing collar.

ALSATIAN MAN FROM OBERSEEBACH, AND WOMEN FROM ASCHBACH AND ENVIRONS OF STRASBOURG

• SECOND HALF OF 19TH CENTURY

The man from Oberseebach has a plain coat over a single-breasted waiscoat with small lapels. He has black breeches with a fly opening. His gaiters are white, and cover the stockings and most of his shoes. He has a wide black hat. His collar is attached to his shirt, and held together with a string-tie pulled through a ring at the front.

The woman from Aschbach is in a bodice and skirt with the high waist of the beginning of the century. The bodice is made of a patterned fabric. The skirt is pleated at the top and worn over a black petticoat with orange bands along the hem. Her neck is filled in with a standing ruffle and covered with a white kerchief. Her coif is padded high at the back.

The woman from near Strasbourg, on the right, has a black petticoat covered by a large green apron. A black embroidered corset is laced over a triangular stomacher that is also embroidered. A large, fringed, coloured neckerchief covers the shoulders and neck. On her head is a black coif typical of her area consisting of a broad bow with long, fringed ends at the back.

GERMAN PROTESTANT MAN AND WOMAN, AND CATHOLIC WOMAN FROM BADEN

• SECOND HALF OF 19TH CENTURY

The man from Baden has a short jacket with the facings buttoned down and a small standing collar. His breeches are embroidered around the front flap. A silver fob hangs from the waist. His heavy black boots reveal his white stockings beneath. Most of the buttons on his scarlet waistcoat are undone, showing his shirt and kerchief. His round fur hat has the flaps tied on top.

His companion's skirt is partially striped; often the front part of the skirt was of a cheaper material because it was covered by an apron. She has a silver-chain girdle around her waist. A corset laces across a stomacher and blouse. In southern Germany, the neck was usually covered with a *koller*, generally square with a round neck, which lay flat on the breast. It was held in place under the arms with cords or ribbons. The figure wears a tall, black cap with lappets, which would sometimes be tied in a bow at the back. The cap itself has a decorated piece at the top of the crown.

The Catholic woman has the same *koller*, blouse and corset, but the stomacher has different decoration and her cap is different. A colourful headcloth covers the cap.

Southern Europe

Italy in the late Middle Ages was still part of the Holy Roman Empire, but during much of this period both the emperor and the pope were largely absent. Their presence had given the region some kind of unity, and their absence led to the growing importance of individual states. By the end of the fourteenth century, power was consolidated between five major powers: Milan, Florence, Venice, the Papal States, and Naples and Sicily. Smaller states of importance included Verona, Mantua and Siena.

The early economic development of Italian towns meant that the middle classes in Italy were richer, better educated and more ambitious than elsewhere. In consequence, there was no great distinction between the life styles of nobles and merchants. There was a constant struggle for power, however, among the ruling élite, and between artisans and small tradesmen, who formed their own guilds.

The prosperity came to an end with the Black Death in the middle of the fourteenth century. Demand for goods fell away, labour costs increased and business activity declined sharply because of the decrease in the population.

Recovery in the fifteenth century saw the various states expanding their territories, creating conflicts with neighbouring powers. Florence, for example, needed a seaport; and Venice wanted to secure its overland trade routes and needed a guaranteed source of food.

Sicily and Naples had been conquered by Aragon in the thirteenth century, creating a long international struggle between France and Spain as the papacy had awarded Naples and Sicily to Charles of Anjou (1226–85). Naples had dynastic interests in Milan at the end of the fifteenth century, and to counter this France was invited into Italy, starting a chain of events that would mean the loss of independence of the Italian peoples until the nineteenth century. Ferdinand of Aragon (1452–1516) intervened in Naples and Sicily, and this eventually led to Spanish Hapsburg domination of Italy that lasted until 1700.

During the later Middle Ages, Italy produced both wool and silk textiles. The wool industry was of great economic importance, and guilds of wool merchants were set up in the twelfth and thirteenth centuries. The Italian silk textiles produced in the fourteenth and fifteenth centuries are better known, however.

Silks were already available in Venice by the year 1000, and Lucca and Sicily had their own silk industries by the twelfth century. Silk-weavers guilds appeared in Florence in 1193, and in Venice and Genoa in the thirteenth century. By 1300, silk manufacture was situated in the north, whereas sericulture was in southern Italy. Lucca was the leading manufacturing centre at that time, but, as it declined, Florence, Venice and Genoa emerged as the important centres of silk weaving. Other towns such as Milan and Siena also produced silk.

Man from Low-Countries in Spanish dress, 1620–30.

(Background image) Italian women, middle to late 15th century.

Italian man, soldier and boy, 15th century (right); Spanish lady, c. 1590–1610 (far right); Venetian senator, 1581 (bottom).

As the focus of world trade moved from the Mediterranean to the Atlantic after the discovery of new territories in the fifteenth century, the economies of the Italian states started to decline.

The unification of the Iberian peninsula preoccupied Christian Spain from the time of the Islamic invasion in the eighth century to the union of Ferdinand of Aragon and Isabella of Castile (1451–1504) in the late fifteenth century. Moorish Granada was captured in 1492, and, in the same year, all Jews who refused to be baptized were expelled. The Inquisition had been set up in 1478, and many thousands fled the country, leaving Spain without many of its most astute citizens and laying it open to exploitation by German and Italian financiers.

The expulsion of the Moors meant Spain could concentrate its resources on conquering more territories in South America and the East Indies. In 1516 Ferdinand of Aragon died, and his grandson Charles (1500–58) was made Holy Roman Emperor in 1519 as Charles V. Because Charles's position as the most powerful ruler in Europe threatened the balance of power, Spain became embroiled in a series of ruinous wars that lasted till the end of the seventeenth century, setting Spain on a course of slow decline. The wars ended when a Bourbon was made king of Spain, as Philip V (1683–1746), in 1700. Spain finally gave up its territories in the Netherlands and Italy in 1713.

Before the Moorish conquest in the eighth century, wool and linen had been the main textile production, while silks were imported from the eastern Mediterranean. The Moors cultivated plants such as flax and cotton, and set up a sericulture. The Arab weavers were highly skilled craftsmen who produced high-quality silks. Leather produced in Cordoba was also an important industry created by the Moors.

Sheep and cattle grazing continued to be a major part of the Castilian economy. The sheep-owners guild, or *Mesta,* was paid for by the government and supported by the merchants who exported their raw wool to Flanders. As the population increased, a growing demand for agricultural products put an end to grazing rights, and the *Mesta* lost its dominant position.

Although some towns expanded their textile and metal industries, they were never as important as the Flemish and Italian cities. Spain essentially still exported raw materials and imported manufactured goods. Silver mining became a major Spanish industry in Mexico and Peru, production being used as payment for imports, to pay off foreign creditors and to fund Spanish armies abroad. Instead of investing in their economy, the Spanish created a rising inflation that affected all European economies.

SOUTHERN EUROPE

ITALIAN SOLDIERS

• 14TH CENTURY

Around 1340, the dress of soldiers and young and active men became much tighter fitting. The change in style from a loose and draped look to a fitted one occurred all over Europe and gradually influenced the dress of everyone. It was probably brought about by the nature of warfare and by developments in textile production. The military fitted and padded jack, which was worn under the armour, played a part in the new fashion since it was the first garment to show the contours of the body. The increasing expertise in tailoring signified a relatively affluent society.

The soldier on the left wears a tunic that is buttoned down the front and has a scalloped hem. The wide sleeves are lined in a contrasting material and could be laced into the shoulders of the outer garment. His hose would have been laced to a tunic underneath. The soldier on the right wears a combination of mail and plate armour. Over this is a surcoat that is belted at the waist, and he wears a heavy fur-lined cloak on top of this. Instead of a full hood of mail, a piece of mail was attached to the base of the steel cap, called the *bascinet*. It has a piece suspended over the chin as seen on the statue of Cangrande della Scala in Verona.

VITTORE PISANI, PAGE AND NEAPOLITAN KNIGHT

• 14TH CENTURY

Vittore Pisani (died 1389) was a Venetian admiral who distinguished himself during the wars between the maritime republics of Venice and Genoa. Pisani and the Neapolitan knight are in armour. The best armour of this period came from Italy, Milan in particular. Both men wear a fitted surcoat: one is fastened with leather straps, the other is perhaps laced at the back. They probably wear a waisted cuirass consisting of a breastplate and backplate. The arms and legs would from now on be protected with pieces of metal rather than mail. The knee pieces, or *poleyns*, now have extensions on the outer sides giving extra protection. From about 1360, a broad belt rested on the hips and was often very decorative. The dagger could be suspended from this or hooked onto the body armour. A shirt of mail was still sometimes worn under the armour, but more often independent pieces of mail were used where they were needed. In the late fourteenth century, mail was typically used to fill the unprotected place between the shin piece and the shoe.

The page in the centre is wearing a breastplate over a patterned jack, or padded doublet. His hose are parti-coloured, a fashion that was associated with heraldry.

YOUNG ITALIAN, ROMAN SENATOR AND TWO VENETIANS

• 14TH CENTURY

The young man on the left has a hooded mantle open along the right side. His hood has a long liripipe falling down the back. Under the mantle he has a short fitted tunic with a broad decorative belt worn low on the hips. As fabric became more elastic, the hose lengthened and the tunic shortened. The Roman senator in the centre has a cape of fur that is cut to fit around the neckline. It is worn over a red gown with side slits for the arms. The slit in the front of the gown reveals that it is lined with fur.

Furs used at this period were from the lynx, marten and squirrel, with sable and ermine the most expensive. The senator's gown is probably lined with vair, from the stomach of the red squirrel, used in imitation of ermine. Linings were usually made separate from the garment so that they could be changed according to the season. The man on the right, with the 'Robin Hood' hat, is probably in travelling attire.

ITALIAN WOMEN

• MID TO LATE 15TH CENTURY

During the fourteenth and fifteenth centuries, sumptuary laws were issued in ever greater numbers as rulers tried to restrict the increasingly rich dress of the middle classes. Women's dress consisted of an undershirt made of linen or occasionally silk. Over that they would wear two or three garments.

The *gamurra* was the main garment worn over the undershirt. It would be of wool or, rarely, silk. It was close fitting, and either with or without sleeves. Over the *gamurra* women wore the *cioppa*, a gown that could be very elaborate. The woman on the right has a horned headdress, which reached Italy from further north towards the middle of the century. Italian women wore lighter veils and showed more of their hair, which was worn long and loose by young girls, as shown by the girl on the left, and plaited around the head by married women; it was often wrapped or plaited with lengths of fabric. A woman's hair was only ever cut when she became a nun or when she was in mourning for a husband.

SOUTHERN EUROPE

FLORENTINE MEN

• SECOND HALF OF 15TH CENTURY

Men's dress consisted of shirt and underpants, doublet and hose, and a long or short outer gown. The hose were laced through the bottom of the doublet. The doublet, or *farsetto,* was lined with linen and had a detachable internal collar, which could be washed. The hose were usually lined with linen and were cut on the cross. Knitted hose were not worn until the sixteenth century.

Lacing, or points, were usually made of silk and worsted braid with metal tips; these tips could be of silver or gold, or some cheaper metal. The two legs of the hose were attached to each other only in the dress of the upper classes; to solve the problem of how to cover the crutch, a separate piece of material was tied on with points. A garment that was open at the sides and put on over the head came into use early in the century. Like the doublet, it was worn by active men and was called a *giornea.* Women could wear it as well. The man on the left could be wearing a *giubba,* a garment like a dressing-gown, lined with fur. It would have been worn over the doublet and hose.

FLORENTINE WOMEN AND GIRL

• LATE 15TH CENTURY

The illustration is based on Ghirlandaio's *Birth of the Virgin,* 1485–90, in Santa Maria Novella in Florence

The girl's striped *cioppa* is seen at the open side of her *giornea.* It has an ornate hem and decorative slashing along the sleeves, with little puffs of linen or silk pulled out. There is a gap at the elbow to make it easier to move the arm in such a tight sleeve. Her *giornea* has heraldic devices woven into the fabric. A woman's *giornea* was generally open at the front. She wears her hair long and uncovered, indicating that she is unmarried.

The woman on the left has covered the back of her hair with a gold hairnet decorated with pearls. She has a long cloak instead of a *giornea.* Shown very clearly on the woman in the middle is how the sleeves were tied into the shoulders of the *cioppa.* She too has covered her head and is probably therefore a married woman.

ITALIAN MEN, BOY AND SOLDIER

• 15TH CENTURY

Only active people, such as the soldier here, wore a doublet and hose on their own – the equivalent of today's sportswear. He has striped hose, which were sometimes a mark of fashion, sometimes the livery of the family the wearer served.

The man on the left is described as a magistrate and could be based on an illustration in the 1590 costume book by Cesare Vecellio. He should be wearing a length of gold fabric, or stole, from his left shoulder, a vestige of the liripipe. He is in a floor-length gown that is lined with ermine. The gown itself is gold, indicating his status. The man in the middle wears on his head the small round *berretto*, the normal headgear in Italy, except in Florence, where the *cappuccio* was worn. This was the Italian version of the chaperon, the hood with its liripipe and padded roll.

ITALIAN MAN, WOMAN AND ARCHER

• 15TH CENTURY

The man from Rimini on the left is in a rich *giornea*, perhaps of velvet, certainly lined with fur. This style appeared early in the fifteenth century. San Bernardino described it in 1422 as being a garment worn only by soldiers and not suitable for civilian wear; he considered it resembled a horse cloth. Under his *giornea* is his *farsetto*, or doublet, which is also of a heavily patterned textile. On his head is a *beretta tonda*, which was usually worn by men in authority.

The archer in the middle is based on a figure from Carpaccio's St Ursula cycle, 1493, in the Accademia in Venice, though the sleeves and the right leg have been altered. He wears a very short doublet with a small pleated skirt at the back only. The laces hanging from his left arm were originally for tying on armour, but by now were mainly decorative.

The figure on the right representing Beatrice d'Este is from a painting of her and her husband, Lodovico il Moro, 1495, in the Brera in Milan. Her style of dress with its stripes and ribbons running down the sleeves is typical of northern Italian dress. The hair is encased in a tube of material and bound around with ribbon; a jewelled cap is attached and sits on the back of the head. It is a hairstyle, first seen in Spain in the middle of the century.

SOUTHERN EUROPE

FLORENTINE WOMEN

• 1581

The figures come from the costume book *Habitus variarum orbis gentium*, by Jean Jacques Boissard, 1581.

The accent was now firmly on the head, shoulders and arms. The bodice was long and from the mid-century pointed. It was laced up and stiffened with canvas or whalebone. The woman on the right does not appear to have any support in her bodice. The early seventeenth-century traveller Fynes Moryson wrote that women wore much linen underneath, because the Italians loved fat women. The sleeves were separate and tied into the bodice at the shoulders. The puffs hiding the lacing are called *spalini* in Italian.

The partlet was the separate infill at the neck, worn with or without a ruff. The woman on the right has an elaborate gold partlet, leaving most of the neck bare. The woman on the left has covered her neck completely with a linen partlet and wears a linen kerchief on top. Moryson described married women wearing a hat with a veil hanging down from the back. Pearl necklaces, gold chains and drop pearl earrings were now in fashion. Pearls were sometimes false ones, often made of glass.

VENETIAN SENATOR AND NOBLEWOMAN

• 1581

Venetian men wore long black gowns, with black stoles over the left shoulder. On ceremonial occasions they wore scarlet cloth. Senators wore crimson velvet; knights wore gold. Moryson wrote that, though many of them wore sumptuous garments, these were hidden under the gowns and only seen by their mistresses.

The figures again come from Boissard's costume book. The woman is dressed in a gown of heavy brocade or velvet. The sleeves have been tied into the shoulders; the ribbons can be seen over the tabbed *spalini*. The waistline is higher than that of the woman above. This is a style particular to Venice. Her neckline is low, but not as low as some commentators would have it. Her hairstyle, with its two horn-shaped knots, is also more subdued than was said to be typical of Venice. Moryson said of Venetian women that they coloured their hair yellow by sun and artifice, and painted their faces and chests white. They were also said to have worn high *chopines* made of wood to keep their feet dry. There was a saying of the time: 'to be tall with wood, fat with rags, red with painting and white with chalk'.

VENETIAN AND MILANESE WOMEN, AND FLORENTINE MAN AND WOMAN

• LATE 16TH CENTURY

The woman on the left is Venetian, her hair more boldly shaped than opposite below. She has a black pleated veil that sits on the centre parting between the two bunches of hair. Her long bodice has a laced-up front that could be purely for decoration. The partlet has a pleated standing collar that would have been starched. The *spalini* are gold like the edging of her bodice. She may be a widow, though women in mourning covered their heads and shoulders with a black veil. The woman next to her is from Milan and has a similar Spanish-influenced hairstyle. Her gown follows the Spanish fashion too; it is tight fitting, closes round the neck and has hanging sleeves. She wears a thick round ruff close up to her chin. Under her outer gown is a bodice and skirt.

The man is also dressed in the Spanish fashion, with a tight round ruff, black doublet and high puffed bonnet. The woman from Florence on the right wears an open gown; the long hanging sleeves have dagged edges, which was rather unusual by this period.

PADUAN STUDENTS AND COUNTRY GIRL

• LATE 16TH CENTURY

The country girl has a wide-brimmed straw hat, which would often have been worn, with or without a caul, on the back of the head. Her corset laces across the front and would have been worn over a loose white smock or a partlet. She has a linen kerchief tucked into the corset. Her skirt is full and shorter than that of women from the town. It has a white skirt over it with some slashed decoration. A linen apron protects the front. On her feet are shoes and wooden pattens.

The Paduan student on the left wears a short Spanish cloak; the one on the right has a fur-lined gown with hanging sleeves. They both wear doublets and long breeches, called Venetians. Their doublets have a slight peascod shape, and they wear small round ruffs. On their heads are the same tall puffed bonnets as in the illustration above. Moryson described the men of Mantua and Ferrara as wearing caps so with gold buttons. He wrote that many men wore jewels, but hidden and only seen by chance, and that Italians wore their hair very short.

SOUTHERN EUROPE

SPANISH NOBLEMAN AND LADY

• c. 1590–1610

It may have been the Burgundian influence on Spanish court dress that created the typical rigid Spanish fashion with its sombre colours. The man here wears a doublet with the distinctive peascod shape, the lower part padded. The Spanish cloak usually had a hood, but other kinds were also worn; this one has a collar, which may be a *ferreruelo*. His short round trunkhose are padded; the codpiece disappeared at around this period. The ruff evolved from the frilled neckband of the 1560s; in Spain it was always worn close to the face. The ruff grew very large after 1590 and a wired support, or *rebato*, became necessary. The high, stiff hats, or toques, were often decorated with feathers.

The woman was perhaps based on Frans Pourbus II's portrait of a young princess in the Uffizi in Florence. She has a farthingale below her skirt; this Spanish fashion was first seen in the fifteenth century. *Verdugado* means 'green wood', and at first hoops of osiers were put on the outside of the petticoat giving it the taut cone shape of the *verdugo*, the hoops eventually being hidden underneath. She is dressed in a stiff and formal manner, with a high closing neck and hanging sleeves that round out at the elbows where a horizontal split is made. In the 1590s, the hair started to point up and, as here, was often decorated with an aigret. The bodice is long at the front and has a slightly concave appearance.

COUPLE FROM THE LOW COUNTRIES IN SPANISH AND FRENCH DRESS

• 1620–30

In 1623, Philip IV issued a pragmatic sanction curbing extravagances in dress. Before 1623, there was much elaborate use of trimming, lace, brocade and embroidery; after 1623, such decoration was prohibited among those below a certain category. At the end of the sixteenth century, the peascod and short trunkhose were succeeded by square-cut jackets and broad-based trunkhose or breeches reaching well down the legs. The high collar supported the plain starched *golilla*, a type of collar seldom seen outside Spain and its dominions.

The man wears a cloak on his left shoulder, which only in Spain continued to be used beyond the middle of the century. By the 1620s, the wide-brimmed hat trimmed with feathers that he carries was worn all over Europe. Twenty years after the 1623 sanction, modest ruffs were still seen on women in Spain, although they were obsolete elsewhere. Open standing collars were seldom worn in Spain. The lady, to be able to wear these luxurious clothes, may be of royal blood. She is in complete contrast to her companion. Instead of the closed Spanish look, she has a deep square neck opening. Her collar is made of the finest lace, and her skirt and bodice are decorated with gold lace. Her gown is perhaps of velvet, and is trimmed with wide bands of silver lace.

WOMEN FROM LAZIO AND MAN FROM NEAPOLITAN APENNINES

• SECOND HALF OF 19TH CENTURY

The women from Genzano in Lazio have full-sleeved embroidered blouses under their corsets, which lace up at the front. The corsets are cut wide and low in front, and the shoulder straps are tied with ribbons. A fichu is tucked into the corset or, as with the woman on the left, a kerchief is tied round the shoulders. Over their plain skirts they wear embroidered aprons. These aprons could be either embroidered, woven or decorated with coloured braids, according to the taste of the wearer. On their heads they wear folded linen cloths, making a flat padded top; the rest of the material hangs down their backs. This type of headdress had appeared in sixteenth-century images of Italian women.

The piper from the mountains is wearing either a sheepskin or a goatskin waistcoat with coloured edgings. He wears this over a jacket and a shirt. On his legs are long breeches bound around the calves with straps. A heavy leather baldrick carries his water-bottle and a bag made from the same skin as his waistcoat. He has a round-brimmed hat on his head.

MEN AND WOMEN FROM VALENCIA AND LEON

• SECOND HALF OF 19TH CENTURY

The man on the left is from Alicante in the province of Valencia. He wears a short black jacket and a waistcoat with tasselled decorations. Underneath, he has a white shirt, with collar attached, which is buttoned up to the neck. He has very wide, white linen breeches that are pleated into the waist and open at the bottom. Around his waist is a blue fringed sash. On his legs are white stockings held under the knee with decorative garters. He has open espadrilles on his feet. A wide-brimmed hat with a pointed crown is on his head. On his left shoulder is a wool blanket decorated along the edge with pompoms.

The woman in front is from Zamora in Leon. Her bodice is almost completely covered by a fringed shawl, which crosses over the front and could be tied behind. Usually, when the sleeves were fitted, it indicated that the bodice was fastened by hooks and eyes. Around her neck is a kerchief on top of the shawl. Her wide skirt is worn over several petticoats, and has bands of lace along the hem and above. She has an ornate apron with a floral design made up from two different fabrics. She has white stockings with a decorative stripe and black leather shoes. Her hair is done up in thick plaits, and she wears large gold earrings.

Western Europe

Relations between the textile industries of France, England and the Low Countries affected the social, political and economic history of each of these countries. Indeed, textile manufacture was one of the most important commercial activities in the region before the Industrial Revolution. Between the twelfth and fifteenth centuries, labour, production and most of the trade was controlled mainly by the guilds.

In the Low Countries, woollen cloth manufacturing was the most important industry from the thirteenth century onwards. England was the chief supplier of raw wool and it was a great loss to the Flemish when several waves of weavers and fullers left for England, where they helped to build up a cloth industry there.

The Black Death in the middle of the fourteenth century halved the populations of France, England and the Low Countries. This, and especially the continuous wars between France and England, caused enormous economic problems.

Holland came into prominence during the second half of fourteenth century, when the Dutch became the main shippers for Europe, taking staple commodities to the Baltic and bringing back goods from the North to Bruges and, when it replaced Bruges in the sixteenth century, Antwerp.

The sixteenth century saw the economic and social upheaval of the Reformation, which affected all three countries. It involved France in a series of internal religious wars, which ended with the Edict of Nantes in 1598, issued by Henry IV (reigned 1589–1610), granting religous tolerance towards the Protestant Huguenots.

Linen had been introduced in the West by the Romans. Flax grew well in northern Europe, and plain linen was woven for domestic consumption in rural areas. Professional linen-damask-weaving workshops were set up in Flanders where the Italian damasks coming into Bruges were copied

The religious struggles, and the uprising against Spain in the Low Countries, caused a large number of people, mainly Protestants, to flee north to the United Provinces from around 1580. Many of the weavers were Protestants. With them went merchants, and the Dutch, who by now were experienced shippers, increased their trade all over Europe and later to east Asia. Amsterdam replaced Antwerp as the principal warehouse and trading centre for all Europe.

England too became a haven for Protestants from the Continent. As the English wool trade declined, merchants had to find new markets for their cloth. Under Elizabeth I (reigned 1558–1603), sailors ventured out of European waters. Trade was established with Russia, and English explorers went in search of new routes to the East Indies. Like Holland, and later France, England formed their East India Company to organize the silk and spice trade with Asia.

English lady, middle of 15th century.

(Background image) Two ladies dressed in the French manner, early 19th century.

In France, Richelieu (1585–1642) promoted economic self-sufficiency. He encouraged the manufacture of silk, linen and wool, among other products. Foreign artisans were persuaded to settle in France and pass on their skills. One of Richelieu's measures was to impose protective tariffs.

English knight, clergyman and lady, 14th century (top left); French peasant, 1620–30 (top right); lady dressed in the French manner, early 19th century (bottom).

The middle of the seventeenth century was blighted by civil and international wars. By 1660, the French had ended their war with Spain, and the English monarchy was restored. By then, all European trade flowed through Amsterdam. French exports were carried in Dutch ships, and Spain and Portugal depended on the Dutch as well. Northern commodities were shipped by them to the Mediterranean and they imported spices and luxury goods from the East. England also relied on Dutch shipping.

In 1685, the Edict of Nantes was revoked by Louis XIV (reigned 1643–1715), causing many Protestants, including many textile workers, to flee to England and Holland. The Huguenot refugees created an important silk industry in Spitalfields in London. Their fine-quality silks would rival those of Lyons.

William and Mary, whose reigns lasted from 1689 to 1702, brought the fashion for Indian chintz with them to England from Holland. Printers in Holland, France and England were soon able to emulate the Indian printed cottons, arousing opposition from the powerful silk and wool industries. France banned printed cottons between 1686 and 1759, and England between 1700 and 1774. Alsace, which was part of Germany, continued printing the cottons and built up a successful industry.

The English printers evaded the prohibition by printing on linen and mixed fabrics for the domestic market, and by exporting the printed cottons to America. England was thus able to continue developing its industry, and introduced machinery into the process. England benefited from the wars on the Continent at the end of the eighteenth century, which occupied its rivals, France and Holland, and it was able to extend its trade worldwide.

France's silk industry in the eighteenth century was the most important in Europe. Lyons dominated, but there were other French cities producing the silks as well. Paris was the centre for gold and silver brocades. Lyons produced velvets, and also simpler fabrics such as damasks, satins and taffetas, which became fashionable at the end of the century. Industry ground to a virtual halt during the French Revolution, but in the early years of the nineteenth century Napoleon I (1769–1821) followed the example of Louis XIV and tried to revive the failing industry with his patronage.

In the nineteenth century, while England was developing the mechanical side of the textile industry, France concentrated on the manufacture of luxury goods, produced mainly by hand. Colour and design were its strengths, and the chemical industry became an important factor in the production of new dyes. The Low Countries still produced textiles, but were left behind by their rivals.

WESTERN EUROPE

ENGLISH KNIGHT AND LADY, CLERGYMAN AND MAN

• 14TH CENTURY

Monumental brasses depict ladies like the one here. Her richly decorated kirtle shows that she is wealthy. The tight sleeves are buttoned to the wrist and reach over the knuckles. Over the kirtle she wears a sideless surcoat with an embroidered or woven edge. Her mantle has a similar edging. Her head and neck are covered by a veil and wimple. The man with her is in a short, padded doublet hidden under a short jacket. His hose are parti-coloured.

The dress of the knight in armour may have been based on the Black Prince, though his surcoat is not the same. The figure is certainly of the period, around the 1360s. Although many examples of mail armour could still be found well into the fourteenth century, it was possible by the 1330s to protect most of the body with plate armour. Under the armour, the knight would wear a close-fitting shirt, short breeches and hose with some padding. He would fit his leg armour, consisting partly of mail and partly of plate, over this. Next would come the top half, the breastplate and backplate, and the defences for the arms; finally he would put on his surcoat and large decorated belt, and his helmet and gauntlets. The helmet, or *bascinet*, was worn with a mail neck defence, the *camail*, laced to it.

ENGLISH WOMAN AND MEN

• 1360s

The woman on the left may have been based on a brass in Ingham Church in Yorkshire of Sir Miles de Stapleton's wife Joan (née Ingham), dated 1364. She wears a cotehardie with long streamers, or tippets, coming from the elbows. Under this is her gown, or kirtle, which is close fitting and would have had a girdle. Its sleeves fit tightly down to the wrist and widen over the knuckles. Buttons were now an important feature of dress. On her head is a veil with a jewelled fillet, and she has looped plaits at the front on either side of her face.

The man in the middle wears a gown that reaches to the calf. It is buttoned down the front and has long sleeves that extend over the knuckles. He has a decorated belt around the waist. Over this is a semi-circular cloak with hood attached. It is fastened on the right shoulder with three buttons. The whole costume is quite plain, but probably made of good-quality woollen cloth. Men generally had centre partings, with the hair reaching down to the neck and below, and forked beards were seen at this period.

The man on the right has a hooded shoulder cape over his gown. A plain leather belt holds a highly decorated purse.

ENGLISH NOBLEMEN AND LADY

• SECOND HALF OF 15TH CENTURY

The lady has a tall headdress typical of the second half of the century with a draped veil over it. Women liked high foreheads and would raise the hairline by plucking. Usually there would be a small black loop at the centre front of the headdress instead of the pointed peak seen here. The truncated headdress was the English form of the high-pointed version seen on the Continent. Over her kirtle she wears a fur-lined gown with large hanging sleeves. The neckline is similar to that of the gown worn in Jan van Eyck's Arnolfini double portrait in the National Gallery in London. A V-shaped neckline was much more usual at this period.

The man in the middle has a doublet with a high collar and over it a short gown with dagged sleeves. Dagging was seen up to the end of the century, though increasingly rarely after the 1440s.

The man on the right has a short gown with a large mantle draped over it. On his head is a chaperon, which developed from the shoulder cape and hood. The liripipe is draped around his shoulders, and a vestige of the shoulder cape sticks out of the top of the padded roll.

ENGLISH KING AND COURTIERS

• END OF 15TH CENTURY

The man on the left is said to be Henry VII. He was crowned king in 1485 and died in 1509. Men's dress changed around 1470 from the wide-shouldered, small-waisted look to a longer slimmer line. Hair was grown to the shoulders, and long gowns reappeared. The large padded head rolls were exchanged for small caps. The king has a long ermine-lined gown with vertical splits halfway up the large sleeves. He wears a blocked-felt bonnet with an upturned brim, to which a jewel was pinned.

The man in the middle is in a long gown, the shape of which is of an earlier style. He still has large, padded shoulders and a high standing collar. On his head is the pre-1570s padded roll and liripipe.

The other two figures were based on grave monuments and are dressed accordingly. The lady is in the ceremonial dress of the first half of the century. The veil and the pleated wimple indicated that she was a widow.

WESTERN EUROPE

HENRY VIII AND ANNE OF CLEVES

• 1530s

Both figures were based on portraits by Hans Holbein. Henry VIII epitomizes the style of his age. The wide shoulders, large chest and codpiece all accentuate his masculinity. His outfit consists of three main components: the doublet, the jerkin with deep U-shaped opening and the gown with large flat ermine collar and puffed-out sleeves. The doublet and jerkin are decorated with embroidery in silver and gold. The doublet is slashed all over with the false puffs of the shirt being pulled through. Large brooches are fixed to the sleeves and the front of his doublet. His flat bonnet has pearl badges attached to the upturned brim and is topped by a white feather. He has a large heavy chain around his shoulders and a second chain with a medallion around his neck. His shoes have very square toes and the tops have slashed decoration.

Anne of Cleves was Henry's fourth wife. Her red velvet dress is in the Nether-German style. It is decorated with gold bands with pearls sewn onto them. The headdress consists of several layers: the coif, the front band of which is embroidered with the motto *A bon fine*, a very fine wired voile cap and a larger cap covered in pearls and jewels, and edged with a jewelled band.

LORD DARNLEY, LADY MARY NEVILLE AND MARY I OF ENGLAND

• SECOND HALF OF 16TH CENTURY

The illustration of Lord Darnley is after an early seventeenth-century print showing him with Mary Queen of Scots. His padded doublet is decorated with slashing and vertical bands. His trunkhose are highly decorated and possibly made of a rich brocade. A slightly puffed-up bonnet is trimmed with a jewelled band and white ostrich feather. The ribbon bows on his shoes are a seventeenth-century feature.

The figure of Lady Mary Neville in the middle was based on a portrait by Hans Eworth of 1559 in the National Portrait Gallery, London. She wears a French hood, a stiffened bonnet that is worn far back, its wide border curving round to the front. A ruched edging trims the lower part of this border, and a decorative metal band the upper part. A pleated veil or a stiff flap hangs down the back.

The illustration of Mary I on the right is after a portrait of the queen by Hans Eworth of 1554, which belonged to the Society of Antiquaries, London. She wears an English version of the French hood, which is flattened across the head. Her velvet brocade gown opens over an underskirt, of which only the front panel would be decorated. It is worn over a farthingale. Her high collar stands out, displaying the white lining. The large fur cuffs reveal gold brocade under-sleeves. They are cut in panes to show the sleeves of the chemise.

ENGLISH WOMEN

• 1560s

These figures are seen in earlier costume books, on maps and in at least one painting of the late sixteenth century.

The woman on the left appears in the earliest known costume book, of 1562. Her distinguishing features are the curiously shaped headdress, the two slanting slashes on her bodice, revealing a second bodice underneath, and the fur-lined muff hanging from her girdle.

The woman in the middle is in a bodice and skirt trimmed with bands of orange with some slashing on the puffed sleeves. She has a white cap over a coif and a white apron.

The country woman on the right is in a gown that opens out over a skirt. She is almost completely covered by a large apron, a kerchief on the shoulders, a chin clout and a ruff around her neck. The chin clout was a diagonally folded square, worn as a practical barrier against dust while walking. On her head she wears a brimmed hat.

ENGLISH WOMEN

• 1640s

These women were based on drawings by Wenceslaus Hollar of the 1640s. The woman on the left has a deep lace border trimming her linen collar. The skirt of her gown has been pinned back for ease of movement and to create the characteristic silhouette of the period. She wears a wide-brimmed straw hat.

The woman a little behind her has a modest triangular collar that is trimmed with lace. Her hairstyle has soft curls falling on either side of the face and a knot at the back of her head. Next to her is the Lord Mayor's wife, of 1649. She still wears a ruff at a time when it was no longer seen in the more fashionable circles. It is worn over a collar that is of the style of the period, as is the rest of her outfit: the boned bodice which laces across a stomacher, the pinned back skirt and the rosettes decorating her gown. On her head is a wide-brimmed hat.

The woman on the right is in winter dress. Around her shoulders she wears a triangular linen collar over a kerchief. The waistline returned to its natural place at this period. The skirt of her gown has been pinned back to show her petticoat beneath. A hood covers much of her head. She wears a fur muff, which was a fashionable accessory.

WESTERN EUROPE

ENGLISH NOBLEMAN AND LADY, AND MIDDLE-CLASS MAN AND WOMAN

• FIRST HALF OF 17TH CENTURY

The aristocrat on the left has short hair. Around his neck is a very plain linen standing collar; his cuffs are trimmed with lace. His doublet is decorated with bands down the sleeves and the front, which has large tabs for its skirt. His large breeches end just above the knee, where the garters are decorated with large rosettes. There are more rosettes at his waist and on his shoes. He carries a sword, hat, gloves and cape.

The lady is in the typical transitional dress of the late 1610s to early 1620s. She has a layered lace-trimmed ruff and a deep neckline. Both the neck and the cuffs are trimmed with lace. The long, hanging sleeves are a feature of this period; she should have a high waistline. A small headdress adds to the height of her hair.

The man and woman in the background are in much plainer clothes. He has a very wide brimmed hat, a pleated linen ruff over a doublet and possibly a cassock. The woman has accentuated her high hairstyle with a feather.

ENGLISH NOBLEMEN AND ROYALIST SOLDIER

• 1640s

The figure on the left was based on a portrait by Van Dyck of William Villiers, Viscount Grandison. He wears the new style of unpadded doublet, which was cut without a waist seam. The sleeves were often slit down their length and the doublet fastened only halfway down the front, exposing the linen shirt underneath. The breeches finish just below the knee and are open legged. Braids run down the outside of the legs and around the bottom edges. He has a large lace-edged collar that spreads over his shoulders. His boots have bucket-shaped tops, his boothose are coloured and end with a lace trim.

The nobleman on the right is dressed in a similar fashion; his breeches are shorter and wider, and decorated with a fringed border below and ribbons along the top. The ribbon bow of his garter shows at the knee. He may be wearing a buff coat, which was a military fashion. The sleeves in this illustration are unusal. He wears the same square-toed boots as Grandison, and both men have butterfly-shaped spur leathers over the instep to which the spurs are attached.

The soldier at the centre has long calf-length boots; these were sometimes laced to the breeches. His buff coat should fasten to the waist, and the skirts to such coats often overlapped slightly at the front. All three men have broad-brimmed hats.

FRENCH GENTLEMAN AND LADY

• MIDDLE OF 15TH CENTURY

The attire of the lady in this illustration was not normal
everyday dress. She is in a rather fanciful costume seen in
representations of historical or mythical figures and saints. Her
silhouette conforms to the period. The high-waisted bodice,
the wide sleeves, the bulky skirts and the wide horned
headdress form part of fifteenth-century dress. However, in the
details it must be considered 'exotic'. The headdress bound in
white linen, the textiles with the star pattern and the wide
chemise sleeves are theatrical.

The man is more conventionally dressed. He wears a short
jacket with heavy pleats, the high collar of the doublet
showing above it. He would normally have put his arms
through the slashes down the sleeves, leaving the bottom half
hanging. His hose are tight, and they are attached to the
doublet. On his feet he has pointed shoes, which he wears with
wooden pattens to keep them out of the dirt. His hair is quite
long, and he has an extraordinarily long feather in his cap.

FRENCH MEN

• SECOND HALF OF 15TH CENTURY

The man on the left wears a long fur-lined gown. The
collar of the doublet shows above it. The sleeves of the
gown are open, and he has a narrow girdle around his waist.
On his head is a small round cap with an upturned brim.

The man with him has a jacket over his doublet. The hanging
sleeves, collar and hem are all trimmed with fur. Both the jacket
and the gown at this period often had deep fan-shaped pleats
front and back. The sleeves would be pleated into the shoulder
seam over large shoulder pads called *maheutres*.

The man on the right is in a long gown with very long-dagged
sleeves. This style of dress was more commmon in the first half
of the century. He has a chaperon on his head, with the liripipe
round his shoulders and the cape protruding at the top.

The man at the back has a flowerpot-shaped hat. He wears a
cloak over his calf-length gown.

WESTERN EUROPE

HENRY D'ALBRET, KING OF NAVARRE AND CLAUDE DE LORRAINE, DUC DE GUISE

• FIRST HALF OF 16TH CENTURY

Both men are in the extra-wide gowns of the first half of the sixteenth century, with the large flat collars falling down the back. Henri d'Albret on the left has a jerkin with a pleated skirt, like Henry VIII, but with a higher square neckline. This neckline is low enough to reveal the shirt underneath. The slashed sleeves may be those of the doublet. The shoes are now very wide and square.

The figure of the Duc de Guise was based on a print. He does not wear a jerkin and so it is possible to see the doublet and hose. The doublet has vertical slashed decoration interspersed with bands of jewelled brooches. The sleeves are treated in the same way. His hose are a good example of *mi-parti*, with the upper hose slashed and banded in different ways. The nether hose differ in that one is plain and the other striped. Both men wear bonnets with feathers.

CHARLES IX OF FRANCE AND HIS WIFE ELEANOR OF AUSTRIA

• 1570s

Charles IX is in doublet and trunkhose. The doublet has a very short skirt and should by now have become slightly peascod shaped. Both he and his queen have thick round ruffs, repeated around his wrists. His trunkhose are quite puffed out, and the panes pushed out to reveal the lining. He has a cape and a brimmed bonnet with a feather.

Eleanor of Austria wears a square-necked gown, with a partlet worked in gold and a ruff above. Her gown is probably made of a rich brocade, and the skirt opens at the front to reveal the petticoat. It is worn over a farthingale. She has wide fur-lined cuffs, which by now are slightly old fashioned. Her headdress is a hood that dips at the centre. Her bodice is covered in brooches and chains, and from her girdle hangs a long pendant chain made of set stones.

FRENCH NOBLEMEN

• 1620–30

These figures were based on engravings by Abraham Bosse. The man in the middle has a cassock draped over his shoulders with loop and button fastenings. The cassock was a loose overcoat with wide sleeves that buttoned down the front. It possibly started as a riding-coat. It was therefore utilitarian but could also be quite elaborate: inventories and contemporary accounts describe embroidered and braided cassocks of velvet, silk and taffeta. He has a falling ruff around his neck.

The man facing him is in a doublet and breeches. The doublet is only buttoned halfway down, showing his shirt below. Around the slightly raised waist is a line of rosettes where the hose would once have been attached, but now this is simply a decorative feature. Instead of tabs, he has a deep skirt, or *basque*. His breeches reach to below the knees, ending with ribbon rosettes tied in bows. His collar is quite deep and trimmed with lace. A cape is draped over his left shoulder.

FRENCH PEASANT, LADY AND GENTLEMAN

• 1620–30

The peasant is in a jacket and full breeches. He has leggings over his shoes and a wide-brimmed hat.

The illustration of the lady was based on a print by Jean de St-Igny. She has raised the outer gown at the sides to reveal her petticoat, which has been decorated with braiding down the front and around the hem. The neckline is wide and low. A plain standing collar fans out behind her and is finished with a pompom at the centre front. She has a fur-lined muff and a small black cap on her head.

The man with her is in doublet and breeches similar to the illustration above. His gloves are probably made of leather and have a fringed edging. Gloves were often scented at this period. His cloak with flat collar has been trimmed to match his breeches.

WESTERN EUROPE

FRENCH NOBLE LADY AND GENTLEMAN

• 1660S–1670S

The woman is in a heavily boned bodice that is cut horizontally along the top. The neckline would be dressed with lace or, as here, with linen and rosette decorations. It ends in front with a long point. The bodice has short sleeves, and the white puffed sleeves seen here are either laced in separately or are part of a chemise. Her skirt opens over a petticoat; often the front was turned back to show off a beautiful lining. Ribbons were the main form of decoration at this period. Her hair is flat at the back and top, with the sides billowing out in small corkscrew curls.

The man is in an early form of coat, which would eventually replace the doublet. It still has the short sleeves of the doublet, but the main body goes down to the knees, almost covering the wide breeches underneath. It buttons all the way down the front. Around his neck he has a bib-shaped lace collar with a small bow tie fastened over it. He has ribbons on his shoulders, which are a vestige of the ties holding the sword belt. On his head he has a broad-brimmed hat covered with feathers. The long shoulder-length curly hair is probably a wig.

FRENCH LADY IN COURT DRESS AND GENTLEMAN

• 1670s–1680s

The lady may be Maria Anna of Bavaria, who was married to the Grand Dauphin of France. She is in court dress, or *grand habit*, which consisted of a long, heavily boned bodice, short cap sleeves and a small fichu around the bare shoulders, The sleeves of the chemise had two layers of frills set in opposite directions. The skirt followed the fashions of the day, and is here pulled back and fixed with jewelled brooches, revealing a petticoat. The textiles of the whole ensemble were rich and elaborate. She has the hairstyle of the 1680s called *hurluberlu*, with short curls, described by Madame de Sévigné as a 'round cabbage head'. It was sometimes softened with long locks as here.

The man is dressed in petticoat breeches, or *rhingraves*. The doublet has now shrunk to well above the natural waist and is worn partly open, revealing the shirt. The sleeves of the doublet have also shortened, and were usually open down the front with the shirt spilling out. Sometimes, as here, they were held together with ribbons and have a lace frill at the bottom. While the doublet has shortened, the breeches have grown very wide, becoming like a divided skirt. They were worn low on the hips and decorated with ribbon loops. His lace collar is bib-shaped.

NOBLE LADIES AND PALACE GUARD

• 1690s

The lady on the left wears a mantua; the lady on the right is in court dress, the figure based on an engraving by André Touvain, *Quatrième Chambre des Apartemens*, 1696.

The mantua, or manto, was a popular garment, for it was much more comfortable than the boned bodices of formal dress. It consisted of a loose gown and an unboned bodice joined to a skirt with a long train, that was worn open to show the petticoat. The fringing on the petticoat, as worn here, replaced the ribbon decorations from about 1685.

On her head, the lady on the left wears a *frelange* headdress. From the 1670s, women had started to have several layers to their headdresses: first ribbons in the curled hair, next a lace-edged bonnet and finally a lace kerchief known as a pinner. From these layers a towering headdress evolved in the 1690s; with the help of false hair and wire frames the *frelange* came into existence. It was not permitted to wear it at court, and the lady on the right has created height with ribbons and jewels rather than the *frelange*.

OFFICER AND MUSKETEER OF THE FRENCH GUARD

• 1680–90

From 1660 onwards, French soldiers were issued with new regulations, and were given improved training and new uniforms. There were several regiments of guards and they were considered the élite. Native-born soldiers formed the French Guards, which was an infantry regiment. Uniforms issued in the 1660s had consisted of grey coats variously braided according to rank. In 1685, a new blue uniform lined with red was introduced. The cuffs and ribbons at the shoulders were also red. The lace was white for the men, whereas the officers had silver embroidery. They had red stockings and black hats, with silver lace, red ribbons and white plumes. From the 1660s, men often preferred to wear cravats instead of collars.

The soldier on the right has tied a long cravat and pinned the twisted ends to his coat. This style was also seen in civilian dress and was called the *Steinkirk* after the Battle of Steinkirk of 1692. Their hair is tied up to prevent it being blown into their faces; this was the beginning of the tie-wigs of the eighteenth century.

WESTERN EUROPE

FRENCH LADY AND GENTLEMAN

• EARLY 18TH CENTURY

During the eighteenth century, the man's suit would consist of a coat, waistcoat, and breeches. Changes in fashion would affect the details only. The coat was close fitting with a flaring skirt that reached to just below the knees. The shape of the skirt was dictated by the pleated vents with stiffened linings at the sides. The front was straight, and dome-shaped buttons ran from the neck to the hem. The coat was usually left open to show the richly decorated waistcoat, which was generally fastened only at the waist to reveal a fine lawn shirt with lace trimmings. The sleeves widened and ended well above the wrist, with buttoned-down cuffs. The lace ruffles of the shirt spilled out below. Men wore knee-breeches throughout the eighteenth century. During the first half of the century, stockings would be pulled over the kneebands. Shoes had square toes and high square heels. The usual type of headwear was the three-cornered cocked hat.

The lady is in a mantua, a gown with an unboned bodice and long train. At the beginning of the century, a fashion was started for covering dress with frills, or furbelows, of different materials. The towering headdress had now started to lean forward.

FRENCH ABBÉ AND SERVANT GIRL

• 1770–85

Both the *abbé* and the servant were based on engravings after Moreau le Jeune in *Monument du Costume*. The plates in this work were first published between 1777 and 1783. The *abbé* is fashionably dressed in a suit partly unbuttoned to reveal the frills of his shirt. By this time, coats have become much skimpier, and the large pleated skirts reduced and shortened. The front curves towards the back to show the breeches, which are now worn over the stockings. The *abbé's* waiscoat is much shorter than the coat. Buttons on both garments run only to the waist. He has powdered his hair or wig, and he has tucked a *chapeau bras* under his arm, a hat that was not meant to be worn on the head. The bands at his neck show him to be a priest.

The girl in the original engraving is selling flowers. She is in a *robe à la française*, a sack-back gown with two box pleats sewn in at the neck that are left loose all the way down the back. The way it is worn, with the ends pulled through the pocket slits, was popular in France throughout the century. She has a cap perched on top of a high 1770s-style wig.

FRENCH GENTLEMAN AND LADY

• 1780

The two figures were based on engravings in *Monument du Costume*. At the back of the coat there are still pleats at the side vents, but they are now no longer stiffened and are much reduced. The backward sloping line of the coat is very clear. The gentleman has a wig with its tail, or *queue*, tied neatly at the back with a black bow. It has two sausage-shaped side curls on either side, and it rises quite high at the front. The wig would have been greased with a pomade and then powdered.

The lady is wearing a *polonaise* gown, with the skirt pulled into three draped puffs. The whole gown is edged with ruched frills. She wears it over a skirt that has been pulled and draped all around. A third striped petticoat is underneath. Stripes became very fashionable in the 1780s. Her wig has sausage-shaped curls arranged down either side and a large looped plait at the back. The wig is very high at this period, with added decorations raising it still more. Parasols were a fashionable accessory.

FRENCH GENTLEMAN AND LADIES

• 1770–80

The man is in a coat that has been cut away still further at the front. It has braided fastenings. His white waistcoat, which is embroidered along the edge, is now quite short. A muslin cravat has been wound around the neck several times and is neatly tied into a bow. From the 1770s, round hats came into fashion, as did the fob ribbons that hang from his waist and large muffs.

The lady in the middle wears a redingote; a garment that was adapted in the 1780s as riding or walking dress from the man's greatcoat. It is here an open robe, with the bodice buttoned, and the skirt open down the front to reveal the petticoat underneath. It has a deep-caped collar, and braided loop and buttons fastenings. The lady on the right is in a *polonaise* gown, with a short, ruched mantle over it. It is short enough to show her shoes underneath. The silhouette of this period is puffed out, from bustle to wig. The lady in the middle has a feather trimming to her wig, which is broad in shape. The lady on the right has a bonnet called a *pouf*, decorated with flowers.

WESTERN EUROPE

FRENCH LADIES AND CHILD

• LATE 1780s TO EARLY 1790s

During the 1770s and 1780s, Anglomania reigned in fashionable circles in France. This was expressed in, among other ways, the adoption of tailored garments in the English style. The lady on the left was based on an engraving of 1787. She is in a later version of the redingote, this one with a large collar and lapels. Her neck is filled with a shirt frill and cravat. Suspended from the heavy belt at her waist are two large fob ribbons. On her head is an exceptionally large headdress, made even taller by two feathers.

The lady in the middle is in a simple muslin gown, known as a chemise gown. This new style had been inspired by various elements, including classical sculpture, children's dress and Oriental dress. It was made popular by a painting of Marie Antoinette so dressed, and it would lead to the simple fashions of the early nineteenth century. The child here has not been dressed in clothes appropriate to her age, as by now had become common. The lady on the right shows the pouter-pigeon silhouette of the 1780s and 1790s.

FRENCH GENTLEMEN AND LADIES

• 1790s

The men are in frock coats. From the 1780s, the frock coat had all but replaced the coat. This was a garment that was originally worn by Englishmen in the country. The men here wear a late 1790s version, with the front cut straight across and the back reduced to two tails. The waistcoat is also cut straight across, but at the natural waistline. Sometimes more than one waistcoat was worn. Both the coat and waistcoat could have collars and revers. The breeches have become long and slim as they have become more exposed. These men still have powdered hair or wigs.

The lady at the front is from a fashion plate in *Modes Parisiennes*. The silhouette of the women of the 1790s is clearly seen here, with the puffed-up breast and the sticking-out bottom: these were achieved with a filmy muslin kerchief tucked into the neck of the garment and bum pads under the skirts at the back. The hair is now much flatter and no longer powdered. The hats have also shrunk.

FRENCH REVOLUTIONARIES

• 1793–4

After the fall of the Bastille in 1789, elected assemblies were set up all over France. After the example of the National Guard in Paris, citizen militia were established elsewhere. The uniform varied according to the location. The tricolour was seen everywhere in civilian and official dress. As the power of the hard-line Left grew, symbols of the Revolution became a common sight in the dress of the followers: the Phrygian cap, or *bonnet rouge*, the working man's jacket and the long trousers.

All three men wear the *bonnet rouge* with tricolour cockade. The man in the middle has the uniform jacket of one of the militia companies over a white waistcoat and blue breeches. The other two are in civilian dress. The man on the left has a tricolour sash across his long greatcoat, which he wears over a red waistcoat and long buff-coloured breeches that have been tucked into boots. The man at the back is in waistcoat and breeches over an open shirt.

FRENCH MAN AND WOMAN

• LATE 1790s

The man was based on figures by Carle Vernet. He is a fashionable young man known as an *Incroyable*. The *Incroyables* were instantly recognizable by their long dishevelled hair, extra-high cravats and tight coats. The square-cut coats have very large lapels and are worn over knee-breeches that have looped ribbons at the base, as in the seventeenth century. The breeches were tight fitting and were usually a little longer than in this illustration.

The woman is in a quilted petticoat, which was worn for most of the century with an overskirt pushed to the back. Her bodice is covered in a puffed-out fichu, but here it is of a striped material in place of the fine muslin illustrated previously. On her head she has a mobcap under a large straw hat decorated with ribbons. She wears a check apron and has pink rosettes on her shoes. The simplicity of her dress, and the printed apron and fichu, suggest that this may be working-class dress, but it is a carefully put-together outfit, and the overall silhouette conforms with contemporary fashion.

WESTERN EUROPE

FRENCH HUSSAR, CAVALRYMAN AND INFANTRYMAN

• 1790s

The French army at this date was in a poor state. There was a shortage of material, and existing uniforms were often either inappropriate or dilapidated. There were, therefore, a great many inconsistencies in the uniforms of the period.

The hussar on the left wears a green dolman braided with white button and loop fastenings. He has slung a yellow pelisse over his shoulder, and his *mirliton* cap has its yellow wing wrapped round it. It is not clear if the contrasting colours were due to the shortages or whether the artist has given the incorrect colouring.

The same problem arises with the illustrations of the other two soldiers, and it is not clear to which regiments they belong. The man in the middle wears spurs and is therefore a cavalryman. He has a blue jacket with red facings and collar over a white waistcoat and breeches. The man on the right is an infantryman. He has a crested helmet on his head with imitation fur on its leather base, which was reinforced with metal bands.

TWO LADIES

• EARLY 19TH CENTURY

Western fashions were strongly influenced by France at this period, and it is not clear if the following three illustrations derived from French sources.

The lady on the left wears a short fur-trimmed jacket ending at the same high waistline as her gown. It has long tight-fitting sleeves that extend over the knuckles. Her gown is of a lightly spotted material. Her low neckline is edged with a frill and has been filled with a fichu. Her hair is in the style of Ancient Greece. Her shoes are flat. The umbrella was now a fashionable item, as was the purse, or reticule; this could be of soft leather or fabric, or perhaps beaded.

The lady on the right is in a slightly later style of dress. The waist of her gown is still very high, but it includes the Romantic touches of a Vandyke ruff, and Elizabethan wings and sleeve decorations. Her hat is tall and rounded, and topped by a ribbon rosette and feathers. The arms are covered with long fingerless gloves. She has a shawl draped around her, which was now becoming an indispensable accessory.

TWO WOMEN

• EARLY 19TH CENTURY

The lady on the left is in a ball dress that has many of the same Romantic touches as the lady in the illustration opposite below. She has a standing pleated ruff, and bands of ribbons decorate her bodice, skirt and sleeves. The front neckline of her bodice is draped with muslin following a seventeenth-century fashion, and the bottom of her skirt has a hem of Vandyke lace with leaves and flowers sewn above it. She has a buckle at the waist and a pearl necklace; her hair is curled and plaited, and decorated with a tiara of roses with an arrow stuck through it.

The dress of the lady on the right also follows Romantic lines. Her pelisse has Vandyke trimming along all the edges. She has a pleated Vandyke collar and cuffs, and her shawl is cut along the same lines. On her head is a tall man's hat decorated with large ribbon rosettes.

TWO MEN

• EARLY 19TH CENTURY

The man on the left is dressed formally in coat and breeches. Coats still had long skirts differing in width at the back, but they were now cut in various ways at the front: straight down, curving outwards or straight across. This man's coat is double-breasted, and it is cut straight across the front. It has a high standing collar and wide lapels, and the striped waistcoat and shirt frill are visible where the coat has been left open. His shirt too has a high collar, and is tied with a cravat. Breeches were now used mainly for formal dress. He carries a huge bicorne hat, which was also part of formal dress; it has been trimmed with feathers. His hair is combed forward *à la Brutus*.

His companion has long striped breeches or pantaloons tucked into hessian boots. His coat or waistcoat is buttoned to the top, with his shirt collar and cravat showing above. His overcoat is known as a carrick. It is a long loose coat with large sleeves and several overlapping shoulder capes.

WESTERN EUROPE

BURGUNDIAN LADIES AND PAGES

• MIDDLE OF 15TH CENTURY

The lady kneeling wears the type of headdress that would be seen for the following twenty years, whereas that of the lady standing behind was becoming outdated. The kneeling lady has a heavy fur-lined gown over her underdress, or kirtle. It has a high waist covered by a broad belt and a very long train. The sleeves are tight and long; they would become tighter as the century wore on. Her towering headdress sits high on her forehead, and it still has two horns. A fine linen veil is draped over it. The two horns would eventually be reduced to one.

The lady behind is in a similar gown, this one lined with black damask or cut velvet. Her headdress is a development of the same padded roll and hood, or chaperon, worn by men. In female headdresses, the padded roll was pushed ever higher and narrower over a tall cap. At the start of this fashion, the hood was wound around the padded roll, and this was eventually formalized into a covering. Both women have ornate necklaces. Rings on all the fingers were much seen at this time.

BURGUNDIAN DUKE AND GENTLEMEN

• MID 15TH CENTURY

The basis of men's dress was still the doublet, which was worn over a shirt. It had a standing collar, and padded chest and shoulders. All three men have very short doublets with the hose tightly laced to them. Over the doublets, the two men on the right wear gowns that have deep regular pleats fanning out to accentuate the broad shoulders and tiny waist. Around the waist are narrow belts or girdles.

The gown of the duke, on the right, has hanging sleeves and is lined with ermine. He has long fine-leather boots that have been laced into the doublet. His hat has an ermine brim, and he wears a heavy chain around his neck. The gown of the man at the centre opens in a deep V to the waist to reveal his doublet underneath. It is not clear whether his headdress is a 'misunderstood' chaperon or a hat with a liripipe.

The man on the left has a sleeveless surcoat over his doublet. His sleeves are of a contrasting material and have probably been laced into the doublet. He has a chaperon with the hood part wound tightly around it.

DUTCH WOMEN

• 1640s

These women were based on engravings by Wenceslaus Hollar. The Netherlands started to play an important role internationally at this time. The small court was led by the Prince of Orange, but it was the rich merchant class that dominated. As conrasted with the court, who wore clothes in the French style, the merchants wore a dark conservative dress made of the most luxurious textiles.

The women are from the bourgeoisie. They wear a simple bodice and skirt with apron. The woman on the left has a jacket over her bodice, with a kerchief around her shoulders. On top is a round white stiffened ruff. Over a white coif, she wears a conical straw hat. The woman next to her has a bodice decorated with stripes. A large round ruff encircles her neck; it sits at a slant and is supported by a wire frame underneath. The woman third from the left is in indoor dress. She has a similar cap, but it is edged with lace, as is her short mantle and apron. She has a jacket under her mantle. The woman on the right is from Antwerp. She wears a *huik*, an all-enveloping cloak that goes over the head; this one ends in a curious pompom on a stem, a fashion seen in the southern Netherlands.

ENGLISH AND FLEMISH MEN

• FIRST HALF OF 17TH CENTURY

The Englishman on the left has a plain linen collar with its strings ending in tassels. A collarpiece called the gorget is under the linen collar. His buff jerkin is quite short and tied in front with cords. The sleeves of his doublet end in turned-back cuffs and are split down their length, showing off his linen shirt. He wears long breeches and wide-topped boots with boothose inside them. He has a hat decorated with feathers and ribbons, and fringed gauntlets.

The Fleming on the right has a lace-edged linen collar round his neck. The sleeves of his doublet are slashed rather theatrically in panes, and there are ribbon rosettes at his shoulders. He wears a buff jerkin and a breastplate; the jerkin has bands around the hem. His breeches are decorated along the side seams. A wide fringed sash is worn around the waist. His wide-brimmed hat is topped with red feathers.

WESTERN EUROPE

NETHERLANDISH LADY AND GENTLEMAN

• FIRST HALF OF 17TH CENTURY

The lady has bodice of blue silk damask with a stiff front that ends in a deep rounded point. Her skirt is made of the same fabric. This is worn over a hooped petticoat, or farthingale. Over these she has a black gown with hanging sleeves. She has a magnificent jewel pinned to her bodice and a simple pearl necklace. Her man's hat with a cocked brim is tilted at a jaunty angle on her head. She has a lace collar and cuffs.

The gentleman is in a black doublet with a more colourful jerkin over it. He wears baggy striped breeches. He, also, has a lace collar and cuffs. A collared cloak is tied around him with cords. He holds a tall-brimmed hat with a long-red feather against his leg. His garters end in a lacy bunch below the knee. The rosettes on his shoes are similarly frilled.

NETHERLANDISH MAN AND WOMAN

• SECOND HALF OF 17TH CENTURY

The bourgeois man's doublet has now shrunk in every direction. The body finishes very high, showing a large expanse of shirt around the waist. The sleeves are short, and a quantity of lace-edged linen spills out. The plain linen bib-shaped collar has large tassels on the end of the strings. He wears his petticoat-breeches low on his hips. A band of ribbon-loops encircles the top, and bunches of loops decorate the sides at the bottom of his breeches and also his shoes. He wears a large cloak on one shoulder. His hair is worn over his shoulders.

His companion is in winter dress. She is masked, possibly for a secret assignation. She has a long, stiff bodice edged around the bottom with tabs. The short sleeves are puffed up and have a lace edge. Her skirt is looped up to reveal her petticoat. She has a fur-lined cape around her shoulders. The muff has a frill along its length. Her cap is tied loosely under the chin.

FRIESIAN WOMAN AND CHILDREN

• SECOND HALF OF 19TH CENTURY

The dress of Friesland conformed to mainstream fashions quite early on. Only in certain areas along the coast of the Zuiderzee, an inland sea that was dammed during the twentieth century, did regional dress continue. In the second half of the eighteenth century, chintz had been a popular fabric all over the northern Netherlands, especially along the coasts of the North Sea and the Zuiderzee. It was there that its use in regional dress continued. The best-known example of the continued wearing of chintz was in Hindeloopen, which was a prosperous town of merchants and seafarers during the seventeenth and eighteenth centuries, with strong trading links with Amsterdam. The dress consists of a tightly laced bodice and skirt that was worn with a variety of jackets: a long coat called a *wentke* and a short jacket. Both were made of chintz lined with white linen.

Both women have a fitted top half, with the skirts flaring out widely by means of gored inserts, accentuated by colourful stitching. The distinctive headdress of the married woman consists of a forward-leaning cylinder that is bound tightly over a cap. It is covered with a starched and specially folded kerchief of check nettle-cloth. The cuffs are of black velvet.

FRIESIAN WOMEN

• SECOND HALF OF 19TH CENTURY

Most Friesians, as described, wore contemporary fashions apart from the headdress, fichu and apron, which were regional elements. The dress of the lady on the left has a bodice with a three-quarter-length skirt and a false front. She has pagoda-style sleeves with false chemise sleeves below, typical of the 1850s and 1860s. The woman on the right has a short-sleeved bodice with false chemise sleeves. Both have a lace-edged fichu; The woman on the left has crossed hers at the front and pinned it with a gold brooch. She has a black lace apron.

On their heads they have the traditional lace caps. These were worn over several layers: first one or more small coifs; then a gold helmet shape that was clamped around the ears; over this, the round lace cap with a lace-edged strip gathered round the sides and back, framing the face. The tradition of ear irons went back to the sixteenth and seventeenth century, when coifs were fixed to the head with a metal clasp. The regional ear irons had decorative pieces on either side that held the cap in place. Most girls of a marriageable age from a well-to-do farming background had a basic set of ring, bracelet and necklace made of gold and garnets to go with their ear irons. Older married women wore more valuable jewellery.

Religious Dress

The religious dress described in this chapter represents only a very small part of this huge subject. The illustrations are exclusively of Roman Catholic vestments, with two examples of monastic dress at the end. In previous chapters, there are a few illustrations of the dress of other denominations.

Ecclesiastical dress and vestments include a wide range of garments and accessories, used in a variety of religious rituals. Some of the garments have gained a symbolic importance that forms part of the liturgy.

In the Early Christian Church, before the fourth century, a priest's dress did not differ from that of his congregation. It was only after the Barbarian invasions of the Roman Empire from the fourth century onwards, when secular fashions changed, that the dress of the clergy was distinguishable from that of the laity. Although the vestments developed mainly from the civilian dress of the Roman Empire, Byzantine and northern influences can also be seen. Roman customs in liturgical dress were spread by missionaries to the churches of the West and North rather than by the imposition of regulations. By the eleventh century, Roman liturgical dress was firmly established in the West, although it developed further during the next three centuries into the form we know today.

The stole derived from the *pallium*, and was a draped garment that evolved into a kind of scarf. The pope conferred it upon archbishops, and later upon bishops, as a symbol of their sharing of his authority. The chasuble, which goes back to the Roman *paenula*, became one of the most important Mass vestments. Originally it was a tent-shaped mantle with an opening at the top for the head, but by the eighth century the sides of the mantle were cut away. Because of the width of the cloth, it had to be pieced together. The resulting seams were covered by woven bands or strips of embroidery called orphreys. Under the chasuble the priest wore several layers. His basic dress was the cassock, which he also wore outside church. For services, over the cassock he would wear an alb, a long white robe bound around the waist by a girdle, and around his neck the white linen amice. On top of the alb he wore two loose robes, the tunicle and the dalmatic. Over his left arm he had the maniple, which was originally a handkerchief.

Below the priest in the hierarchy were the deacon and the subdeacon. Their characteristic vestments were the dalmatic and the tunicle, which they wore over a cassock. The colours of their dalmatic and tunicle usually matched the priest's chasuble.

The cope, not worn at Mass, was a processional garment. The origins of the cope are not clear, but it, too, may derive from the *paenula*. Although the shape of the chasuble

Bishop, 16th–17th century.

(Background image) Byzantine bishop, deacon and priest, 6th–12th century.

changed over the centuries, the shape of the cope remains much as it was at the end of the Middle Ages. Open at the front, the two sides of the cope are held together by a metal clasp called a morse. The surplice was a late modification of the alb. By the fourteenth century, it had become established as a choral or processional garment.

The undervestments, such as the amice and the alb, were usually made of linen. This made them easier to wash, which was essential for these white garments. The outer vestments were often of precious materials and frequently decorated with magnificent embroidery.

During the Middle Ages, the colours of the liturgical vestments varied according to local custom. However, in 1570, after the Council of Trent, Pope Pius V set out new regulations as to which colours were to be used and when. These regulations have remained virtually unchanged. White or silver, the colour of joy, purity and innocence, are used for Easter and Christmas, and for the festivals of saints except those of the remembrance of martyrs, when red is used. Red signifies blood and fire, and is also used for Whitsun. Purple is the colour of preparation and penitence. It is worn during Lent and Advent, and on other penitential days. Green is a neutral colour, used when there is no specific celebration. Gold can be used instead of any of these colours. Black is always used for funerals and Masses for the dead.

Monastic dress developed during the sixth century. St Benedict set down the rules at that time for communal monasticism and for the standardization of the dress of monks. Monastic garments were based on rural dress and would typically include a habit with a belt or girdle, a hood, or cowl, and a protective apron called a scapular. The different orders showed slight variations in shape and colour, but the basic garments were the same.

Benedictine nuns, 19th century (left); Subdeacon and chorister, 16th– 17th century (top); Franciscan monks, 19th century (bottom).

RELIGIOUS DRESS

BYZANTINE BISHOP, DEACON AND PRIEST

• 6TH–12TH CENTURY

It is not certain when bishop, deacon and priest became distinctive offices, separate from other Christian worshippers. What is known is that before the end of the third century they did not wear distinctive liturgical dress. In the late Roman Empire, a tunic with a *pallium* would have been worn by the middle and upper classes in Judaea and elsewhere. The Roman tunic was essentially an indoor garment, usually of wool and worn with a linen undershirt. During the Barbarian invasions, from the fourth century, fashions in secular dress changed, while the vestments of the clergy did not. At ceremonies, both the Romans and the Jews wore white clothes, and this custom continued with the Christians. Garments changed their shape and function, and became more elaborate and precious. The clothes as vestments acquired a sacred and symbolic function they had not had before.

The bishop in the centre has a *paenula*, now a chasuble, over a heavily decorated dalmatic; this in turn is worn over a linen tunic. His stole can be seen hanging below the dalmatic. Over the chasuble he has a *pallium*. The deacon on the left wears a dalmatic with *clavi*, with a chasuble over it. From the eighth century, only priests and bishops were permitted to wear the chasuble. The priest on the right is in a tunic with *clavi*, a patterned dalmatic, and a chasuble and *pallium*. At this period, the clergy still went bare headed.

FRANKISH BISHOP, PRIEST AND MONK

• 11TH CENTURY

Monasticism did not become a communal movement until the sixth century, with the Rule of St Benedict. Even after this, however, it took some time for standardization to become established.

It is not possible to say to which order the monk on the left belongs. He wears an outer gown with a hood, the front of which is connected to the back with St Benedict's stitches, as they were known. The chasuble worn by the bishop, in the middle, is decorated with round patches on his shoulders, and a collar that could be embroidered or woven with gold thread. Around his neck is the amice, a square white linen cloth used from around the tenth century to protect the precious embroidery of the vestments. Under his chasuble is a dalmatic with a deep, decorated hem. Below this can be seen the fringed stole and the tunic, or alb. On his head he wears an early form of mitre. It is a soft cap with a decorated band around it and one crossing over it from front to back. Two fringed lappets hang down from the back. His pastoral staff, or crozier, is always held in the left hand. The priest is in alb and dalmatic. By this period, the clergy were tonsured.

BISHOPS

• 16TH–17TH CENTURY

The bishop on the left is in a cope; the bishop on the right is in a chasuble. The cope is a semi-circular cape based on a protective garment worn during the late Roman Empire. It first appeared as a processional garment around the eighth, century, worn by the clergy and the choir. Its use increased up until the thirteenth century, when, except at the celebration of the Mass, it became the main vestment worn by the priest. It could be extremely valuable, depending on the cloth and on the embroidered or woven bands, called orphreys, of the garment. It usually fastened with a decorative clasp called a morse. The original hood of the Roman cape still remains here in the shape of a triangle or shield on the back. The shape of the chasuble changed as its decoration became more elaborate. When it became too heavy and stiff for the priest to be able to raise his arms, the sides began to be cut away. The mitres were now high and stiff, and decorated with orphreys.

The bishop on the right has a maniple hanging from his left arm that originally developed from a kind of handkerchief. Gloves along with the crozier were part of the bishop's dress.

DEACON, SUBDEACON AND CHOIRISTER

• 16TH–17TH CENTURY

The deacon and the subdeacon assisted the priest. Instead of the priest's chasuble, they wore respectively the dalmatic and the tunicle at Mass. These both had the same cross shape and from the late Middle Ages were almost indistinguishable. The colour and fabric of the dalmatic and tunicle conformed with that of the chasuble. Both garments were decorated with the two *clavi* from shoulders to hem, now called orphreys. These could be richly ornamented. Both garments had wide sleeves and were often edged with fringing. Like the chasuble, they became increasingly ornate and heavy, and therefore narrower. The dalmatic had always had slits up its sides, but these became longer, and both garments became shorter.

The priest, on the right, is dressed in an alb, a long garment that was always worn with a girdle with fringed or tasselled ends, known as the *cingulum*. His stole is crossed in front, which is how priests would wear it. The alb and amice have square patches called apparels, which could be woven or embroidered like the orphreys. The deacon always wears his stole on his left shoulder. The subdeacon does not wear a stole or amice. The choirboy has a surplice over a cassock.

RELIGIOUS DRESS

POPE IN ECCLESIASTICAL VESTMENTS AND SWISS GUARD

• 17TH CENTURY

Papal dress consisted of the amice around the neck and the alb, which was girded by a *cingulum*. The stole was worn around the neck, with the ends falling straight down the front, and the maniple on the left arm; the tunicle and the dalmatic were worn under the chasuble; the *pallium* was put on over the chasuble; pontifical stockings and sandals were worn on the feet. By the late sixteenth century, the apparels on the alb were being replaced by lace. The pope's gloves were always white.

The standing pope is in processional dress of tiara and cope. The headdress probably developed from the Phrygian cap. Known as a tiara, it consists of three diadems with two lappets hanging from the back. His cope has a border decorated with saints, and it is fastened by a morse. Under the cope, the pope has an elaborate stole and an alb with a deep hem of lace; it is girded with a *cingulum* with tasselled ends. He has a cross staff in his left hand. The seated pope has a red fur-lined skullcap on his head, and a fur-lined hooded cape called a *mozetta* over a cassock and a lace rochet, a kind of alb that was shorter and not girded.

CARDINAL, PRELATE AND CHAMBERLAIN

• 17TH CENTURY

The cardinal ranks below the pope in the Roman Catholic Church, and it is from among the cardinals that a new pope is chosen. He can be a bishop, priest or deacon.

The cardinal, in the middle, is dressed in a red cassock with a train and close-fitting sleeves. Over this is a mantle with two slits for the arms and a fur-lined hood. This would be a poncho-shaped mantle with a hole for the head, the front part held up by the arms. On his head is the cardinal's hat, with the distinctive cords with tasselled ends. The red hat was first granted to cardinals by Innocent IV in the thirteenth century. Instead of embroidery, lace was used, and rich fabrics in larger quantities than before. The train has become longer.

The prelate on his right is in a cassock and a short alb, with a deep lace hem and cuffs. On his shoulders is a *mozetta*. Over this is a sleeveless garment that is the *mantellone*, worn by papal prelates. His head is covered with a skullcap.

FRANCISCAN MONKS

• 19TH CENTURY

The rules set down by St Benedict in the sixth century resulted in an increased standardization of monastic dress. It was essentially rural dress: breeches, tunic or habit, with a belt or girdle, hood and protective apron, or scapular, worn over the shoulders. For dignity's sake, the tunic was worn long; the cowl, put on over this, was a hooded mantle that varied in shape and size. The dress was meant to be functional: it had to serve as protection against the cold and yet be unrestricting for manual work.

The Franciscan order was founded in the thirteenth century by St Francis of Assisi. At first, the monks wore a coarse grey habit, which by the fifteenth century had been replaced by a brown one; they continued to be known as the Grey Friars, however. The most characteristic element of Franciscan dress, other than the colour, is the cord belt. The monks were not allowed to wear shoes, and had bare feet or wore sandals.

BENEDICTINE NUNS

• 19TH CENTURY

The Benedictine order was founded in the first half of the sixth century. According to the prescriptions of St Benedict, the nuns' dress was to consist of undyed black garments, a sleeved habit fastened with a leather belt, a hooded sleeveless cowl, a scapular, shoes and stockings. These came in winter and summer weights. It was essentially the dress of all married women and widows of the Middle Ages.

Women wore a tunic with a wide-sleeved loose garment called a surcoat. Instead of the monks' hood, they wore the wimple and head-veil. The wimple was a piece of linen draped round the chin, with the ends pinned on top of the head; a fillet of stiffened linen held it in place. It was worn with a veil. This fashion lasted till the early fourteenth century, but survived in the dress of widows and nuns. On the left is a novice, who is in plain civilian dress, but in the black of the order. With her are two nuns in summer and winter habits.

FASHIONS OF THE PAST
GLOSSARY

Alb A long white linen tunic with sleeves that from the 6th century was worn only as part of liturgical dress.

Baldrick An ornamented belt or sash worn across the body to carry a sword or pouch.

Batik Javanese fabric with the design printed by a process in which the part not to be dyed is covered by wax.

Brandenburg A type of fastening on an overgarment with loops and braided buttons.

Caftan A simple sleeved overgarment of ancient Asian origin, brought to eastern Europe following the spread of the Mongolian and Ottoman empires. Versions include the Polish *zupan* and Russian *doloman* and *zipun*. It is also part of Middle Eastern and African dress.

Carrick A heavy coachman's overcoat adapted for gentleman's wear, double- breasted and with one or more capes.

Cassock In ecclesiastical dress, a full-length garment, usually with a standing collar. In military and civilian dress, a long coat or cloak, buttoned down the front, worn in the 16th and 17th centuries.

Chlamys A woollen mantle of Dorian origin, pinned at the neck or shoulder, worn mainly by the young men of Ancient Greece.

Chaperon A Medieval form of hood.

Chemise A light undergarment with long full sleeves, often gathered into the neckband.

Chiton A linen or cotton tunic of Ionian origin, worn long by the women of Ancient Greece and knee length by the men from 600 BC.

Cioppa A gown worn over the *gamurra* by Italian women during the Renaissance, made of a rich material and often embroidered.

Codpiece A piece of cloth or pouch covering the front opening of men's hose. In the 16th century, it assumed an exaggeratedly protruberant form.

Coif A soft cap fitting tightly to the head and often tied under the chin.

Cotehardie A Medieval outer tunic or gown. The female version was long with a low neckline.

Dagging A Medieval form of ornament in which the edges of a garment were given a jagged edge.

Dalmatic A T-shaped tunic with wide sleeves and decorated with *clavi*, vertical bands at both sides of the garment, front and back, originally denoting the status of Roman dignitaries. It continued in use in ecclesiastical dress.

Djellaba A voluminous outer garment worn throughout the Middle East.

Doublet Originally a quilted garment worn by soldiers, and worn on the upper body by European men from the 14th until the late 17th century. It generally fastened at the centre front with buttons and could be with or without sleeves.

Farthingale A hooped skirt that first appeared as a bell-shaped underskirt in late 15th-century Spain, the *vertugado*. In the late 16th century, a padded roll was worn at the waist to increase the fullness of the silhouette.

Fichu A neckcloth for the throat and shoulders.

Frock coat A man's outer garment with a turned-down collar, worn from the mid-17th century, later with the front cut away at the waist.

Fustanella A white pleated skirt worn by men in the Balkans.

Gamurra A long-sleeved undergarment worn under the *cioppa* by Italian women during the Renaissance.

Himation A mantle worn especially by the men of Ancient Greece, larger than the *chlamys* and draped in various ways.

Gorget A garment covering the neck and throat; also a piece of armour.

Hose Covering for the legs, with or without an integrated foot piece, made from knitted or woven material.

Houppelande A full over-gown with wide sleeves, generally belted and of any length, worn by men and women from the late 14th to the late 15th century.

Huque A flowing overgarment, open at the sides.

Jerkin A jacket, generally sleeveless, worn over a doublet.

Kimono The traditional garment worn by Japanese men and women made from seven pieces of silk sewn together with a seam at the centre back.

Liripipe The lengthened part, or tail, of a Medieval hood, which was sometimes padded.

Mantua A loose gown with an unboned bodice, worn by women from the mid-17th to the mid-18th century over a corset and petticoat.

Palla A cloak worn by the women of Ancient Rome.

Pallium The outer garment worn by the men and women of Ancient Greece. Made from a square or rectangle of wool, it was fastened and draped in various ways. It continued in use in ecclesiastical dress

Partlet A detachable collar or yoke, fashionable in the later 16th century.

Peascod The padded paunch shape characteristic of men's doublets in southern Europe in the second half of the 16th century.

Pelisse A wide padded mantle, fur edged and often fur lined, of the 18th and 19th centuries.

Peplos A wool garment worn by the women of Ancient Greece consisting of a rectangle of cloth with the top folded over, joined at the shoulders and girded at the waist.

Pluderhose Full German style of breeches, with silk linings spilling out between the broad panes.

Pu fu The traditional outer garment worn by Chinese men bearing a square patch signifying the wearer's status.

Redingote A double-breasted robe with revers and collar, and a low opening, adapted from men's dress and fashionable for women from the mid-18th to the mid-19th century.

Rhingraves Petticoat breeches, often with loops and ruffles, fashionable for men in the late 17th century.

Sarafan A long sleeveless gown worn by women in Russia.

Sari The traditional dress of the women of India consisting of a length of cloth wound and draped around the body.

Sarong A cloth wrapped around the body to form a skirt, worn by men and women in such countries as Burma, Java and Ceylon.

Spencer A short jacket with long sleeves derived from men's dress, worn by women in the early 19th century.

Steinkirk A cravat worn with the ends tucked into a buttonhole in the late 17th century.

Stola A long loose garment of linen or wool worn by the women of Ancient Rome, the equivalent of the Greek *chiton*.

Stomacher A stiff decorative panel ending in a point at the waist, forming the front of the bodice.

Surcoat A long overgarment, with or without sleeves, worn by men and women.

Toga The principal outer garment deriving from the Etruscan *tebenna* and worn by the men of Ancient Rome, the equivalent of the Greek *pallium*. It was generally made from white wool, and the manner of draping it became more complicated in the course of time. The decoration signified the wearer's status.

Trunkhose Covering for the upper leg, from the waist to the knee.

Tucker A decorative yoke infilling the open neck of a woman's bodice.

Tunic A garment, long or short and with or without sleeves, that was slipped on over the head. The Egyptian *kalasiris*, the Greek *chiton* and the Roman *tunica* were early versions.

Vandyke A type of decoration with deep points as appears in the paintings of Van Dyck.

Wimple The headdress of Medieval women comprising a cloth draped around the head to frame the face, held in place with a band over the brow, worn with a veil.

FASHIONS OF THE PAST
BIBLIOGRAPHY

For a subject that spreads itself as wide as the one in this volume, there is much to read.
The books listed below are the ones used as reference for the text and at the
same time the ones most accessible to the general reader.

Arnold, J., *Queen Elizabeth's Wardrobe Unlock'd* (Leeds, 1985)

Ashelford, Jane, *Dress in the Age of Elizabeth I* (London, 1988)

Beaulieu, M., and Bayle, J., *Le Costume en Bourgogne de Philippe le Hardi à Charles le Témeraire* (Paris, 1956)

Braudel, Fernand, *Civilization and Capitalism* (London, 1981)

Buck, Anne, *Dress in Eighteenth-century England* (London, 1979)

Cunnington, C. W. and P., *Handbook of English Medieval Costume* (London, 1952)

Cunnington, C. W. and P., *Handbook of English Costume in the 16th Century* (London, 1954)

Cunnington, C. W. and P., *Handbook of English Costume in the 17th Century* (London, 1955)

Eichler, Ulrike, *Münchener Bilderbogen* (Munich, 1974)

Evans, J., *Dress in Medieval France* (Oxford, 1952)

Harris, Jennifer (ed.), *5000 Years of Textiles* (London, 1993)

Hottenroth, Friedrich, *Handbuch der deutschen Tracht* (Stuttgart, 1896)

Marly, Diana de, *Louis XIV and Versailles* (London, 1987)

Mayo, Janet, *A History of Ecclesiastical Dress* (London, 1984)

Newton, S. M., *Fashion in the Age of the Black Prince* (Woodbridge, 1980)

Newton, S. M., *The Dress of the Venetians 1495-1525* (London, 1988)

Norris, Herbert, *Costume and Fashion* (Great Britain, 1924)

Paine, Sheila, *Embroidered Textiles* (London, 1990)

Pipponier, F., *Costume et Vie Sociale: La cour d'Anjou XIV–XV siècle*
(Paris and La Haye, 1970)

Rajab, Jehan, *Palestinian Costume* (London, 1989)

Ribeiro, Aileen, *Dress in Eighteenth-century Europe* (London, 1984)

Ribeiro, Aileen, *The Art of Dress* (London, 1994)

Rubens, Alfred, *Jewish Costume* (Great Britain, 1967)

Scott, Margaret, *Late Gothic Europe* (London, 1980)

Snowden, James, *The Folk Dress of Europe* (London, 1979)

Zander-Seidel, Jutta, *Textiler Hausrat* (Munich, 1990)

FASHIONS OF THE PAST
ACKNOWLEDGEMENTS

The author would like to thank Dr Aileen Ribiero at the Courtald institute, Mary Schoeser,
Dr Jane Bridgeman, Elizabeth Dawson, Sumie Tani, Marieke de Winkel, Dr Konrad Vanja at the Museum für
Volkskunde in Berlin, Dr Adelheid Rasche at the Kunstbibliothek in Berlin,
Putriga Ampaipan at the Royal Thai Embassy and Lyn Avery.